THE
CHICKPEA
FLOUR
COOKBOOK

THE
CHICKPEA
FLOUR
COOKBOOK

Healthy Gluten-Free and
Grain-Free Recipes to Power
Every Meal of the Day

CAMILLA V. SAULSBURY

Published by:
Lake Isle Press, Inc.
2095 Broadway, Suite 301
New York, NY 10023
(212) 273-0796
E-mail: info@lakeislepress.com

Distributed to the trade by:
National Book Network, Inc.
4501 Forbes Boulevard, Suite 200
Lanham, MD 20706
1(800) 462-6420
www.nbnbooks.com

Library of Congress Control Number: 2015940856

ISBN-13: 978-1-891105-56-2
ISBN-10: 1-891105-56-6

Book and cover design: Laura Palese

Editors: Jennifer Sit and Pimpila Thanaporn

This book is available at special sales discounts for bulk purchases as premiums
or special editions, including customized covers. For more information, contact the
publisher at (212) 273-0796 or by e-mail: info@lakeislepress.com

First edition
Printed in China

10 9 8 7 6 5 4 3 2 1

To My Parents,
Daniel & Charlotte

contents

introduction

Gluten-free food is experiencing meteoric popularity.

It's hardly a scenario anyone anticipated just a short while ago. When gluten-free foods and cookbooks first appeared on store shelves a decade ago, the target audience was highly specialized: individuals diagnosed with celiac disease, wheat intolerance, or gluten intolerance. At present, diagnosed celiacs represent less than 0.1 percent of the population, with an actual number (diagnosed or undiagnosed) estimated at 1 percent of the total population; individuals with some sort of wheat or gluten intolerance represent 6 percent to 7 percent of the population.

The goal of the recipes and resulting foods was likewise niche driven: eliminate gluten from recipes and re-create traditional foods (in particular, grain-based baked goods) without it. To achieve these ends, the gluten-free standard was soon defined by a laundry list of highly refined grain flours, starches with little or no nutrition (e.g., cornstarch and tapioca starch), and added gums, such as xanthan gum and guar gum. It hardly sounded like a recipe for mainstream appeal, let alone zeal.

Yet more than one-third of all American adults now report that they want to cut down on or be free of gluten in their diets.[1] The principal explanation for this monumental shift is that gluten-free products are perceived as healthier. Whether individuals are looking to avoid genetically modified grains, lose or control weight, deal with allergies, manage health issues, or just live a healthier lifestyle overall, following a gluten-free eating plan is now considered a mainstream approach to healthy eating.

Gluten-Free 2.0

The second wave of gluten-free marks an exciting shift in priorities for cooking and baking, both for those who cannot have gluten, as well as anyone and everyone who chooses to remove gluten from their diets. The emphasis is moving away from time-intensive, extensive-ingredient recipes that are short on flavor and nutrients to recipes that are:

- **Nutrient-dense:** Skip the fillers and gums; instead, focus on whole foods that are naturally gluten-free and rich in macro- and micronutrients (e.g., healthful fats, proteins, fiber, vitamins, and minerals). Non-GMO ingredients are a huge bonus.

- **Simple to prepare:** Think familiar methods without the fuss, and easy-to-follow instructions that make the recipe nearly foolproof.

- **Minimalist:** A short list of ingredients is key (unlike gluten-free 1.0, where combinations of fifteen-ingredient recipes, multiple gluten-free flours, and fillers were *de rigueur* to make even the simplest of recipes work).

- **Allergen-free or low-allergen:** The same consumers who are turning to gluten-free recipes are also interested in avoiding other high-allergen ingredients, such as tree nuts, soy, dairy, eggs, and in some cases, all grains.

- **Great-tasting:** Poor taste and texture just won't cut it; consumers are not willing to compromise great health with bad taste. The new focus is on foods that taste just as good, if not better, than those with gluten, thanks to innovative flavor combinations and techniques.

---

[1] *The 2014 data comes from NPD Group, a leading global information company, who began asking the question in 2009. The question is posed in their Dieting Monitor survey, which continually tracks (on a bi-weekly basis) top-of-mind dieting and nutrition-related issues facing consumers.*

Chickpea Flour Saves the Day

The aforementioned list of attributes may sound insurmountable. That is, until you consider chickpea flour.

Chickpea flour—also known as garbanzo bean flour, ceci flour, chana, gram flour, or besan—is an all-natural, grain-free flour made from finely ground dried chickpeas. It is anything but a fad; it has been in use for centuries in rustic, everyday recipes throughout Southeast Asia, the Middle East, and Northern Africa, as well as regions of Italy, France, and Spain. It appears in myriad preparations, including everything from flatbreads, pancakes, dumplings, and soy-free tofu to creamy sweets.

Now chickpea flour is slowly garnering star status in the Western food world for its unique flavor and flexibility across an even broader range of recipes. It is nothing short of a gluten-free godsend to home cooks interested in crafting gluten-free foods for the following reasons:

- **Ease of use and versatility:** Like all-purpose wheat flour, chickpea flour is incredibly versatile. It can be used to create baked goods (e.g., breads, pizza crusts, muffins, and crackers) and main dishes (soups, stews, meatless burgers, and eggless quiches and omelets), as well as desserts, snacks, and sauces.

- **Low cost:** Chickpea flour is very inexpensive. Make that *cheap*. This is in stark contrast to the high price tags on other gluten-free flours and flour blends, some of which cost upwards of $10 per pound. The fact that chickpea flour can be used solo—no starches, gums, or other gluten-free flours—further ensures lower costs overall. Chickpea flour is available in well-stocked grocery stores and health food stores, from online retailers, and also in many Middle Eastern and Indian food stores. Alternatively, you can make it yourself from dried chickpeas in a matter of minutes.

- **Grain-free and high in protein:** Chickpea flour is more than a gluten-free flour, it is also free of all grains and high in protein. One cup of chickpea flour contains 22 grams of protein, twice as much protein as the same amount of whole-wheat flour and six times the amount of protein in all-purpose wheat flour. Moreover, it is a higher-quality protein than the protein in wheat and other grains because it has significant amounts of all the essential amino acids except sulfur-containing amino acids, making it very close to meat protein.

- **Rich in vitamins and minerals:** Chickpea flour is an excellent source of folate, containing seven times more folate than whole-wheat flour. It also contains exceptional levels of vitamin B-6, iron, magnesium, and potassium. Chickpeas are one of the best plant sources of selenium, an important but often overlooked micronutrient. Selenium is an antioxidant, meaning it helps protect cells from oxidation, which may be a contributing factor to cancer. Selenium also assists in the body's absorption of vitamin E, which helps prevent cataracts from forming and plays an important role in the prevention of macular degeneration. Further, selenium aids the body in processing and using proteins that are consumed. Hair is primarily composed of proteins, so when the body is able to better process the proteins, hair growth will follow.

- **High-fiber carbohydrate:** Chickpeas make a seriously fiber-loaded flour: 1 cup (120 g) of chickpea flour supplies 20 grams of dietary fiber, a remarkable contrast to the 2.6 grams of fiber found in one cup of all-purpose wheat flour. The carbohydrates in chickpea flour are resistant starch, which means that they do not spike blood sugar levels and are extremely beneficial to overall digestive health. Any carbohydrate-containing food has some effect on your blood sugar. After you eat a meal, your body breaks the carbohydrates from your food into glucose, a simple sugar. This glucose then enters your bloodstream, so it can circulate throughout your body and provide fuel to your cells. High-glycemic index (GI) foods, such as refined wheat flours and refined gluten-free grain flours, lead to rapid blood sugar spikes and subsequent crashes that leave you hungry and irritable shortly after eating. Chickpea flour, a low-GI food, absorbs more slowly, preventing blood sugar spikes and crashes, so you feel satisfied for longer after you have eaten.

- **Great taste and texture:** Chickpeas have a natural buttery, nutty flavor and texture; the same holds true for the flour. It can make crispy foods extra crispy and creamy foods extra creamy. Further, it yields delectable baked goods that, depending on the recipe, are either remarkably similar in texture and flavor to their counterparts made with all-purpose flour or entirely unique, with a taste and crumb like nothing else.

- **Hypoallergenic:** Chickpeas are considered a hypoallergenic food, making chickpea flour one of the lowest allergen flours available. The term *hypoallergenic foods*, or *low-allergenicity foods*—refer to foods that are least likely to cause allergic reactions in humans. They are typically recommended as first foods for babies, but they are also used in allergy-avoidance diets (sometimes called elimination diets), which are designed to identify specific foods that may be causing adverse reactions.

- **Non-GMO:** Chickpeas are a highly sustainable crop worldwide and, to date, have undergone little to no genetic modification. Chickpeas, along with lentils and field pea crops, are very sustainable because they do not require nitrogen-based fertilizers, which are derived from fossil fuels.

As compelling as the above reasons are, my last three reasons explain why you will want to make every recipe in this collection again and again. First, they are absolutely and unfailingly delicious. Second, they are loaded with nutrient-rich, complementary ingredients. And last, they are simple to prepare.

My recipes honor several classics from around the world—for example, Italian *farinata*, Provençal *panisse*, and Indian roti—but the majority of the dishes represent new and exciting uses for this multipurpose flour. Think Brown Sugar Banana Bread (page 78), Garlic and Sweet Chile Chickpea Chips (page 90), Black Bean and Mango Empanadas (page 138), Coconut Chickpea Onion Rings (page 110), and Blueberry Crisp (page 169). Additionally, as unusual as it may sound, chickpea flour is a unique stand-in for eggs, and hence you'll find my egg-free interpretations of scrambles, omelets, and Spanish tortillas, as well as a garlicky chickpea aioli and a velvety lemon curd.

Lastly, in addition to being gluten-free, all of the recipes are free of nuts, grains, and soy, and the vast majority of recipes in the collection are also either naturally vegan (dairy- and egg-free) or include a simple modification to make them so. In short, this is meant to be a collection for everyone to savor.

I hope you'll enjoy the many uses and charms of chickpea flour as you cook your way through the book and that these recipes, as well as chickpea flour in general, will soon be part of your everyday repertoire.

the chickpea flour pantry

I'm not a fan of fussy, exotic ingredients.

Hence the overwhelming majority of pantry items mentioned are readily available at well-stocked supermarkets. A few less-than-usual ingredients make an appearance, too, but not without careful consideration. I have only included specialty ingredients (for example, psyllium husk) that are critical to a recipe's success, are versatile enough to be used in multiple recipes, and are extra special in the areas of nutrition and taste.

A quick word of caution when stocking your pantry: be sure to check labels to ensure that the product you are buying—from the chickpea flour to the chocolate chips—is certified gluten-free. Gluten is found in many obvious places (breads and bread products), but it is also hidden in thousands of products you would never think to suspect. Reading labels is critically important, as is becoming familiar with the names of potential gluten ingredients. Celiac organizations such as the National Foundation for Celiac Awareness, Celiac.com, the Center for Celiac Research, and the Celiac Disease Center offer information about hidden gluten ingredients on their websites.

Chickpea Flour

Chickpea flour is made by grinding chickpeas to a fine consistency. It looks and feels like all-purpose wheat flour and can be used in a broad range of baking recipes, from desserts to muffins to breads. But unlike any other flour, chickpea flour can also be used to make dips, spreads, and egg-free egg dishes.

Chickpea flour does not need gums (such as xanthan gum or guar gum) in order for it to work in baking recipes, a feature that is particularly appealing to anyone interested in gluten-free baking, incorporating nutritious non-wheat flours into their diets, or creating baked goods that fit into a high-protein, low-carbohydrate diet.

Chickpea flour has a distinctive earthy, nutty flavor and scent. When the uncooked flour is mixed into batters, it may smell faintly of beans. But fear not! In sweet recipes, any hints of bean flavor virtually disappear as the flour cooks, while in savory recipes, the subtle nuttiness of the flour enhances and highlights the other ingredients. The more familiar you become with chickpea flour, the more you will love the way it works in recipes and complements a wide variety of ingredients and flavors.

When baking with chickpea flour, keep in mind that it tends to absorb more liquid than wheat and other grain flours. Recipes for quick breads and muffins, for example, tend to benefit from the addition of an extra egg (or psyllium "egg"), additional liquid, or leavening. Follow the recipes in this collection for guidelines, and then have fun experimenting with your own recipes and variations.

BUYING CHICKPEA FLOUR

Chickpea flour is available from a wide variety of purveyors. It is available in health food stores, natural food grocery stores, and in the health food sections of well-stocked supermarkets. These are the best places to find packages of the flour that are certified gluten-free. The flour is typically labeled as chickpea flour or garbanzo bean flour and is shelved with other specialty flours or in the gluten-free foods section of the store.

If 100% gluten-free certification is not a requirement for your diet, even more opportunities for purchase are available. For the best prices on chickpea flour, look in the bulk foods section of natural food grocery stores. It is also available in international markets, including Italian markets (where it may be labeled ceci flour), Middle Eastern markets, and Indian and Southeast Asian grocers (where it may be labeled gram flour, besan, or chana). The chickpea flour in the latter stores is sometimes sold pre-toasted. All of the recipes in this collection call for untoasted flour, but you can experiment with toasted flour in any of the recipes. The resulting flavor will have nuances of toasted nuts or seeds.

A list of resources for buying chickpea flour from online purveyors is provided in the Ingredient Sources (see page 171).

STORING CHICKPEA FLOUR

For the best flavor and freshness, always check the expiration date on the package. Store the flour in a tightly sealed zipper-top plastic bag or airtight container in the refrigerator for up to 6 months or in the freezer for up to 12 months. Let the cold flour return to room temperature before using it.

Measuring Chickpea Flour

It is very important to measure chickpea flour accurately, especially in recipes for baked goods. The best way to measure is with a kitchen scale, which is why I have added measurements in grams for the chickpea flour amounts in all of the recipes.

If you choose to measure using traditional measuring cups, note that the technique is slightly different than measuring all-purpose flour. All-purpose wheat flour must be lightly spooned into dry measuring cups for accurate measurement. By contrast, chickpea flour requires lightly packing the flour into the appropriate-size dry measuring cup to achieve an accurate volume and weight. Simply spoon the flour into the cup and gently press down on the flour with the back of the spoon. Repeat until the cup is full to slightly overflowing, and then slide a straight-edged utensil across the top to level off the extra.

Make Your Own Chickpea Flour

You can make your own chickpea flour with whole, dried chickpeas, using a grain mill, a clean coffee or spice grinder, or a high-speed blender. Keep in mind that it will be very, very noisy; not the best choice at 10 p.m., or when children and pets are napping.

If you're using a grain mill, follow the directions for grinding chickpeas into flour. If you're using a high-speed blender, place 1½ to 2 cups of dried chickpeas in the blender. Process on high speed until the beans are finely and evenly ground.

If using a coffee or spice grinder, place ¼ cup of dried chickpeas in the grinder (adding any more will overload the grinder and prevent the beans from being ground to a fine consistency). Using on-off pulses, process, shaking the grinder every few pulses to ensure an even grind, until the beans are finely and evenly ground. Repeat with more chickpeas until you have the desired amount of flour.

Once you have ground the chickpeas into flour, sift it through a fine-mesh sieve to remove any larger or uneven pieces. Store the flour in the same manner as store-bought chickpea flour.

TOASTING CHICKPEA FLOUR

Chickpea flour is transformed upon toasting. The color changes from bisque to caramel and the flavor is akin to finely ground nuts or seeds. Toasted chickpea flour is used in a host of Southeast Asian dishes and, as previously noted, can be purchased pre-toasted in Southeast Asian grocery stores. It is also used as a condiment in Middle Eastern cooking and is ideal for thickening and enriching sauces, gravies, soups, and stews in a matter of minutes.

To toast chickpea flour, heat a large cast iron (or other heavy skillet) over medium-high heat. Add the flour; cook and stir for 6 minutes, lowering the heat to medium if the flour begins to brown too quickly in spots. Lower the heat to medium or medium-low; continue to cook, stirring, for 4 to 6 minutes longer, until the flour is golden brown and fragrant. Transfer the flour to a rimmed baking sheet or wide bowl and let it cool to room temperature.

Alternatively, toast the flour in the oven. Place a large, rimmed baking sheet in the oven; preheat the oven to 350°F. Remove the sheet from the oven and evenly sprinkle 2 to 3 cups of chickpea flour on it. Shake the pan slightly so that the flour settles into an even layer. Return the sheet to the oven and bake for 5 minutes. Open the oven door and stir the flour, particularly stirring the flour at the edges toward the center. Continue to bake, stirring the flour at 2-minute intervals (it will take one or two more rounds) or until the flour is golden and fragrant. Transfer the flour to a cool rimmed baking sheet or wide bowl and let it cool to room temperature.

Store the toasted flour in the same manner as untoasted chickpea flour.

Eggs and Egg Substitutes

EGGS

The chickpea flour recipes in this book that call for eggs were tested with large eggs. Select clean, fresh eggs—preferably organic—that have been handled properly and refrigerated. Do not use dirty, cracked, or leaking eggs, or eggs that have a bad odor or unnatural color when cracked open; they may have become contaminated with harmful bacteria, such as salmonella.

PSYLLIUM "EGGS"

You may be unfamiliar with psyllium husk, but once you try it, you'll likely use it exclusively for all of your egg-free baking. It is essential for replacing eggs in chickpea flour baking.

Psyllium (*Plantago ovata*) is an annual herb that is grown in India and some European countries. Its seeds contain large quantities of mucilage, a type of soluble fiber that absorbs water to produce a thick gel. It's this thick gel that works wonders as an egg replacement and is essential in gluten-free, vegan baked goods; without it, your results will literally crumble. Please note that it cannot be replaced with ground flaxseeds or other egg replacers.

To make a psyllium "egg," mix 2 teaspoons of whole psyllium husks with 3 tablespoons water and 1½ teaspoons neutral vegetable oil; let the mixture stand for 5 minutes to thicken or gel. It is important to add the oil to the mixture to make up for the fat that is present in egg yolks.

Psyllium husk can be purchased at health food stores, pharmacies, and online health food purveyors. Be sure to select whole psyllium husks (preferably organic), not psyllium husk powder.

Dairy and Nondairy Milks

DAIRY MILK

The recipes in this book that call for dairy milk were tested with low-fat milk. However, equal amounts of skim (nonfat) milk or whole milk can be used in its place without compromising the recipes, so use the dairy milk you have on hand. Alternatively, use one of the nondairy milk options listed below.

BUTTERMILK

Commercially prepared buttermilk has a delicious and distinctive tang. It is made by culturing 1 percent milk with bacteria. When added to baked goods, it yields a tender, moist result and a slightly buttery flavor.

If you don't have buttermilk, it's easy to make a substitute. Mix 1 tablespoon lemon juice, white vinegar, or cider vinegar into 1 cup milk. Let it stand for at least 15 minutes before using, to allow the milk to curdle (i.e., the mixture will appear somewhat lumpy). Do not strain the mixture; use the curdled bits and all. Any extra can be stored in the refrigerator for the same amount of time as the milk from which it was made.

YOGURT

Yogurt, like buttermilk, is acidic and adds a distinctive tang to recipes. It tenderizes and lightens chickpea baked goods, in particular. Plain, low-fat yogurt was used throughout, but any fat content will do. Do not, however, use Greek yogurt where plain yogurt is specified; the difference in texture and level of liquid will lead to very different results.

NONDAIRY MILKS

Using nondairy milk in place of dairy milk is a simple way to make many of the recipes in this collection vegan as well as accessible to those who are lactose intolerant or allergic to dairy. Although nondairy milks are available in a variety of flavors, opt for plain when substituting for milk in any of the recipes in this collection. The following options are grain-, nut-, and soy-free, but you can use any nondairy milk of your choosing.

Hemp Milk Hemp milk is made from hemp seeds, water, and a touch of sweetener. It is rich in healthy omega-3 fatty acids, protein, and essential vitamins and minerals. Because of its neutral taste, it can be used in a range of sweet and savory dishes.

Flax Milk In comparison to other nondairy milks, flax milk has a flavor and texture most similar to cow's milk. Commercial flax milk is made from cold-pressed flaxseed oil mixed with water. Flax milk is high in omega-3 fatty acids and calcium. It is also a good source of vitamin A, vitamin B-12, and vitamin D.

You can make your own flax milk by combining ⅓ cup raw whole flaxseeds with 6 cups filtered water in a blender and blending on high for 1 minute. Strain the mixture through cheesecloth then refrigerate in a tightly covered container for 3 to 5 days.

Sunflower Seed Milk Sunflower milk has a rich texture and a faint sunflower-seed taste. It is a good source of calcium and also has small amounts of vitamin A and iron. To make sunflower milk, soak 1 cup raw sunflower seeds in filtered water overnight. Drain the seeds, add them to a blender with 3 cups water, and blend on high until smooth. Strain through cheesecloth. Store in the refrigerator for 3 to 5 days in a tightly covered container. Shake well before using. The same method may also be used to make milk with sesame seeds or pumpkin seeds.

Coconut Milk All of the recipes calling for coconut milk in this collection specify full-fat (typically 17 percent fat or slightly higher) coconut milk. It is a rich, full-flavor, snow-white liquid produced from grating and pressing fresh coconut meat. Be careful not to use "light" coconut milk or coconut milk beverage in place of the full-fat coconut milk; both have much lower fat contents, and using them will lead to markedly different results, especially in baked goods.

If you choose to use coconut milk where nondairy milk is specified, use half full-fat coconut milk, half water (for example, for 1 cup of nondairy milk, use ½ cup full-fat coconut milk mixed with ½ cup water).

Coconut milk is available in cans and, occasionally, in Tetra Paks. It remains mostly liquid at room temperature. Some of the liquid and fat separate, even at room temperature, hence it is important to stir or gently whisk the milk upon opening until it is blended smooth. Transfer any unused coconut milk to an airtight container and refrigerate for up to 5 days, or freeze for up to 6 months.

Nondairy Buttermilk Nondairy buttermilk is made in the exact same manner as the dairy substitute for buttermilk. Mix 1 tablespoon lemon juice, white vinegar, or cider vinegar into 1 cup nondairy milk. Let stand for at least 15 minutes before using, to allow the milk to curdle. Any extra can be stored in the refrigerator for the same amount of time as the milk from which it was made.

Fats and Oils

OLIVE OIL

Olive oil is a monounsaturated oil that is prized for its use in a wide range of dishes. Extra-virgin olive oil is the cold-pressed result of the first pressing of the olives and is considered the finest and fruitiest of the olive oils. The subtle nuances of extra-virgin olive oil shine best when it is uncooked, whether in salad dressings or drizzled on top of soup. Consider using olive oil simply labeled "olive oil"—produced from additional pressings of the olives and far less expensive than extra-virgin—for general cooking purposes.

VEGETABLE OIL

"Vegetable oil" refers to any neutral, plant-based oil that is liquid at room temperature. Examples include grapeseed oil, safflower oil, or sunflower oil. Opt for the type of oil that suits your needs and preferences but strongly consider selecting oils that are:

- **Expeller-pressed or cold-pressed** (expeller-pressed oils are pressed simply by crushing the seeds, while cold-pressed oils are expeller-pressed oils that are produced in a heat-controlled environment)

- **High in healthful unsaturated fats** (no more than 7 percent saturated fat)

VIRGIN COCONUT OIL

Virgin coconut oil is oil harvested from fresh, young coconuts with a minimal amount of processing. A bonus of this minimal processing is that the oil retains a delicate coconut scent.

Unlike other plant oils that are prone to rancidity and must be refrigerated, coconut oil can be stored at room temperature. In cool regions, during winter months, or in the refrigerator, the oil is solid, but in warm climates, such as the tropical regions in which coconuts grow, it remains a clear liquid year-round. When kept at room temperature, the oil will fluctuate from liquid to solid; this is completely normal and, unlike other oils, it does not affect the oil's quality.

It is simple to scrape out a teaspoon or tablespoon of coconut oil when it is solid, but when a larger amount is needed for a recipe it is easier to melt the coconut oil before measuring. As noted above, it does not harm the coconut oil to be warmed to a liquid state, so you can quickly liquefy the entire jar of coconut oil. To do this, simply hold the sealed jar under warm running water, or place in a bowl of warm water, until there is enough liquid coconut oil to measure out.

NONSTICK COOKING SPRAY

Nonstick cooking spray is a convenient option for quickly greasing pans when baking with chickpea flour. Opt for the type of cooking spray that suits your needs and preferences but read the label and strongly consider selecting varieties that clearly indicate that they are (1) made with high-quality oils (e.g., expeller-pressed or cold-pressed oils) and (2) use compressed gas to expel the propellant, which means that no hydrocarbons are released into the environment.

Chemical Leaveners

Chemical leaveners lighten dough (i.e., cause it to rise). The two varieties used in the baking recipes in this collection are baking powder and baking soda.

GRAIN-FREE BAKING POWDER

Baking powder is a chemical leavening agent made from a blend of alkali (sodium bicarbonate, known commonly as baking soda) and acid (most commonly calcium acid phosphate, sodium aluminum sulfate, or cream of tartar), plus some form of starch to absorb any moisture so a reaction does not take place until a liquid is added. When baking powder is combined with a liquid, a chemical reaction produces carbon dioxide, which is trapped in tiny air pockets in the dough or batter. Heat releases additional carbon dioxide and expands the trapped gas and air to create steam. The pressure expands the air pockets, thus expanding the food.

The alkali and acid components of baking powder are naturally gluten-free, but most commercial brands use cornstarch for the starch component of the mix. The good news is that grain-free baking powder is easy to prepare. To make 1 cup of baking powder, combine ½ cup cream of tartar, ¼ cup baking soda, and ¼ cup arrowroot or tapioca starch. Store the baking powder in an airtight container in a cool, dark place for up to 6 months.

Testing the Potency of Baking Powder

Baking powder loses its potency over time. To test your supply before using it in a recipe, pour ⅓ cup hot water over ½ teaspoon baking powder in a cup. The mixture should bubble vigorously. If it does not, toss the baking powder out and purchase a new container.

BAKING SODA

Baking soda is a chemical leavener consisting of bicarbonate of soda. It is alkaline in nature and, when combined with an acidic ingredient such as buttermilk, yogurt, citrus juice, honey, or molasses, it creates carbon dioxide bubbles, giving baked goods a dramatic rise. Baking soda is naturally gluten-free.

Testing the Potency of Baking Soda

There is no accurate way to test the potency of baking soda. As a general rule, though, replace the box every 6 months for optimal freshness. Write the date the box was opened on the front for an easy reminder.

Seeds and Seed Butters

Seeds and seed butters are very nutritious. In addition to being excellent sources of protein, nuts and seeds contain vitamins, minerals, fiber, and essential fatty acids (such as omega-3 and omega-6).

Toasting seeds deepens their flavor and makes them extra crisp. To toast whole pepitas or sunflower seeds, spread the amount needed for the recipe on a rimmed baking sheet. Bake in a preheated 350°F oven for 5 to 8 minutes, until golden and fragrant. Alternatively, toast the seeds in a dry skillet over low heat, stirring constantly for 2 to 4 minutes, until fragrant. Transfer the toasted seeds to a plate and let them cool before chopping.

FLAXSEED MEAL (GROUND FLAXSEEDS)

Flaxseeds, also known as linseeds, are one of the richest sources of alpha-linolenic acid (ALA), an omega-3 poly-unsaturated fatty acid. To reap the most benefits from the seeds, they must be ground into meal. Pre-ground flaxseeds, typically labeled "flaxseed meal" are readily available in supermarkets and health food stores. Alternatively, whole flaxseeds can be ground into fine meal using a spice or coffee grinder.

Flaxseeds are available in two varieties: brown or golden. Despite the difference in color (and, in many cases, price), the two are interchangeable and offer the same health benefits. Flaxseeds—both whole and ground—are prone to rancidity due to their high oil content, so store them in an airtight container in the refrigerator for up to 5 months or in the freezer for up to 8 months for optimal freshness.

PEPITAS (GREEN PUMPKIN SEEDS)

Pepitas are flat, green, hulled pumpkin seeds. They are a good source of protein, fiber, and healthy fats and are a go-to substitute for nuts in almost any recipe. Pepitas are delicious raw, but their flavor (naturally sweet and nutty) really shines when they are toasted.

CHIA SEEDS

Once a staple of the Aztec diet, chia seeds—an edible seed from the desert plant *Salvia hispanica*—rival flaxseeds for their high levels of omega-3 fatty acids. They are also a great source of calcium, protein, manganese, copper, iron, niacin, phosphorous, zinc, and fiber. Unlike flaxseeds, chia seeds do not require grinding to make their nutrients available. Additionally, they can be stored at room temperature, in an airtight container, for several years without becoming rancid.

HEMP HEARTS (SHELLED HEMP SEEDS)

Hemp hearts are the shelled, tan, and pale green seeds of hemp plants. The seeds have a soft texture reminiscent of pine nuts and a delicate flavor that makes them versatile for all kinds of recipes and uses, both sweet and savory. The tiny seeds contain all ten essential amino acids in an easily digestible form; a mere two tablespoons of hemp hearts contain seven grams of protein, equivalent to the amount of protein in a large boiled egg. Hemp hearts are very high in omega-3 and omega-6 fatty acids, and are also rich in B vitamins, folic acid, phosphorus, potassium, magnesium, and calcium.

SHELLED SUNFLOWER SEEDS

Mild, nutty sunflower seeds are highly nutritious and have a smooth texture that is complementary to countless other flavors. They are a great source of energy and unsaturated fat and also contain calcium, protein, iron, and zinc. The recipes in this collection call for seeds that have been removed from their shells.

SESAME SEEDS

Petite, yet packed with flavor, sesame seeds add a distinctive nutty flavor and delicate crunch to both sweet and savory recipes. Their flavor increases exponentially when they are toasted. Sesame

Go Nuts

If you are free of any nut allergies or sensitivities, you can use an equal amount of chopped nuts (e.g., almonds, pecans, or walnuts) in place of sunflower seeds and pepitas. Similarly, an equal amount of unsweetened, minimally refined nut butters (e.g., peanut, almond, or cashew) can be used in place of seed butter in the same manner as store-bought chickpea flour.

seeds are also highly nutritious: they are an excellent source of copper, a very good source of manganese, and a good source of magnesium, calcium, phosphorus, iron, zinc, molybdenum, and selenium.

SEED BUTTERS

Seed butters, such as tahini, sunflower seed butter, and hemp seed butter have unique, rich flavor profiles that enhance a multitude of chickpea flour recipes. They are an excellent alternative to nut butters for those with tree-nut allergies or sensitivities. Minimally refined, unsweetened seed butters are increasingly available at well-stocked supermarkets, food co-ops, and natural food stores. They may be used interchangeably in any recipe calling for nut or seed butter, unless otherwise specified. Make sure to use smooth seed butters throughout, not chunky. Store opened jars or containers in the refrigerator.

Minimally Processed Sweeteners

Minimally processed sweeteners are closer to their whole form than refined sweeteners, which have most or all of their natural vitamins and minerals removed during the refining process. But the benefits don't stop there. Minimally processed sweeteners offer a broader spectrum of flavors than refined sugar; I find that these nuances make scaling back on the total amount of sugar in a recipe much easier.

NATURAL CANE SUGAR

Natural cane sugar goes by many different names: raw cane sugar, whole cane sugar, dried cane juice, evaporated cane sugar, and evaporated cane juice. What matters is the definition: juice of the sugar cane plant that is evaporated and crystallized without use of chemicals. Natural cane sugars are available in a wide range of colors and textures, but the recipes in this collection were tested with a pale blond, fine-grained variety unless otherwise specified. Natural cane sugar is readily available in the baking section, alongside other sugars, of most supermarkets.

COCONUT PALM SUGAR

Coconut palm sugar is an all-natural, unrefined sugar made from coconut nectar. Once the coconut nectar is collected, it is air-dried to form a crystalline sugar that looks and tastes much like brown sugar with a very faint coconut flavor. It dissolves and melts the same as other sugars and can be used measure for measure in place of white or brown sugar.

HONEY

Honey is an all-natural, liquid sweetener manufactured entirely by honeybees. The bees gather nectar from a wide variety of flowers and concentrate the nectar in beehives. Honey is available in many colors and varieties, but the recipes in this collection were tested using a mild, light-colored honey. Feel free to use any variety of honey that you prefer. Store unopened containers of honey at room temperature. After opening, store honey in the refrigerator to protect against mold. Honey will keep indefinitely when stored properly.

MAPLE SYRUP

Maple syrup is a thick, all-natural, liquid sweetener made by boiling the xylem sap from sugar maple, red maple, and black maple trees. Store unopened containers of maple syrup at room temperature. After opening, store maple syrup in the refrigerator to protect against mold. Maple syrup will keep indefinitely when stored properly.

Dried Fruit

Whenever possible, opt for organic dried fruit with no added sweeteners or in the case of dried cranberries, fruit juice–sweetened. The following are my top picks:

- **Raisins (both dark and golden)**
- **Dried apricots**
- **Dried cherries**
- **Dried cranberries**
- **Dried blueberries**
- **Prunes (dried plums)**
- **Dried figs**
- **Dried currants (sometimes labeled Zante currants)**
- **Dried, unsweetened mangoes**
- **Dried, unsweetened pineapple**

Softening Dried Fruit in Warm Water

Dried fruit can vary tremendously when it comes to moistness and softness. If your fruit is particularly hard and/or dry, give it a quick soak—from 2 to 10 minutes, depending on the toughness of the fruit—in warm (not hot) water. Drain the fruit and pat it dry between paper towels before using.

Fresh Dates

Fresh dates have a caramel-like flavor reminiscent of molasses and brown sugar. Fresh dates can be found in the fresh produce section of the grocery store, either in packages or in bulk. Opt for dates that are plump-looking; it is okay if they are slightly wrinkled, but they shouldn't feel hard.

If fresh dates are unavailable, whole dried dates can be used in their place. Packages of whole dried dates can be found where raisins and other dried fruits are shelved in the supermarket. Soak the dried dates in warm water following the previous tip before measuring for the recipe.

Chocolate and Cocoa

GLUTEN-FREE CHOCOLATE

Gluten-free chocolate was difficult to find just a few years ago. These days, manufacturers are making it easy to identify and select a wide range of gluten-free chocolates in bars, blocks, and chips, even at the local supermarket. The best way to identify gluten-free chocolate is to check (and double-check) the label. Bars of gluten-free chocolate tend to be easier to find than gluten-free chocolate chips. If necessary, use 3 ounces chocolate, chopped, for every ½ cup of chocolate chips. See Ingredient Sources (page 171) for options, including sources for gluten-free chocolate chips.

COCOA POWDER

Cocoa powder is a natural by-product of roasted cacao beans after the cocoa butter has been removed. The crumbly bean bits are ground, and the result is natural cocoa powder. Although cocoa powders vary by brand, they typically have a brownish-red hue and a deep chocolate flavor. Dutch process cocoa powder undergoes an additional step: chemical washing in a potassium carbonite solution that neutralizes cocoa powder's natural acidity. The resulting color is darker than natural cocoa powder, sometimes almost black. The recipes in this collection use natural cocoa powder, not Dutch process.

Flavorings

Chickpea flour is a blank canvas that welcomes flavor, from subtle to bold and everything in between. Elevating chickpea flour dishes to exceptional levels of deliciousness can be as easy as creating a harmonious balance of simple flavorings—even if you're just adding salt and pepper. Here are my top recommendations for ingredients that will make the ordinary extraordinary:

FINE SEA SALT

The recipes in this collection were tested using fine-grain sea salt. I prefer fine sea salt because it has naturally occurring trace minerals and is produced without chemicals and other additives. However, an equal amount of conventional table salt can be used in its place.

BLACK PEPPER

Black pepper is made by grinding black peppercorns, which have been picked when the berries are not quite ripe, and then dried until they shrivel and the skin turns dark brown to black. Black pepper has a strong, slightly hot flavor, with a hint of sweetness.

SPICES AND DRIED HERBS

Spices and dried herbs can turn the simplest of meals into masterpieces. They should be stored in light- and airproof containers, away from direct sunlight and heat, to preserve their flavors.

Food co-ops, health food stores, and mail-order sources that sell herbs and spices in bulk are all excellent options for purchasing very fresh, organic spices and dried herbs, often at a low cost.

With ground spices and dried herbs, freshness is everything. To determine whether a ground spice or dried herb is fresh, open the container and sniff. A strong fragrance means it is still acceptable for use.

Note that ground spices, not whole, are used throughout this collection. Here are my favorite ground spices and dried herbs:

Ground Spices

- **Black pepper (cracked and ground)**
- **Cardamom**
- **Cayenne pepper (also labeled "ground red pepper")**
- **Chili powder**
- **Chipotle chile powder**
- **Cinnamon**
- **Coriander**

- **Cumin**
- **Garam masala**
- **Ginger**
- **Hot pepper flakes**
- **Nutmeg**
- **Smoked paprika (both hot and sweet)**

Dried Herbs

- **Oregano**
- **Rosemary**
- **Rubbed sage**
- **Thyme**

FRESH HERBS

Fresh herbs add an aromatic backbone to chickpea flour recipes. I use them liberally in many recipes in this collection. When added during the cooking process, they willingly surrender their flavors and aromas in minutes. Alternatively, you can add them as a final flourish for a bright note of fresh flavor and color.

Flat-leaf parsley, cilantro, and chives are readily available and inexpensive, and they store well in the produce bin of the refrigerator, so keep them on hand year-round. Basil, mint, and thyme are best in the spring and summer, when they are in season in your own garden or at the farmers' market.

CITRUS ZEST

Zest is the colored outer layer of citrus peel. The oils in zest are intense in flavor. Use a zester, a Microplane-style grater, or the small holes of a box grater to grate zest. Avoid grating the white layer (pith) just below the zest, as it is very bitter.

GLUTEN-FREE VANILLA EXTRACT

Pure vanilla extract is made by macerating vanilla beans in a mixture of alcohol and water. The mixture is then aged for several months, or longer, depending on the quality of the extract. Look for brands that are clearly marked on the package as gluten-free.

INSTANT ESPRESSO POWDER

Instant espresso powder is very strong instant coffee made from dark roasted coffee. It is readily available in well-stocked supermarkets where coffee is shelved. If it is unavailable, use double the amount of instant coffee powder in its place.

DIJON MUSTARD

Dijon mustard adds depth of flavor to a wide range of dishes. It is most commonly used in this collection for salad dressing because it facilitates the emulsification of oil and vinegar.

CIDER VINEGAR

Cider vinegar is made from the juice of crushed apples. After the juice is collected, it is allowed to age in wooden barrels.

RED WINE VINEGAR

Red wine vinegar is produced by fermenting red wine in wooden barrels. This produces acetic acid, which gives red wine vinegar its distinctive taste. Red wine vinegar has a characteristic dark red color and red wine flavor.

WHITE WINE VINEGAR

White wine vinegar is a moderately tangy vinegar made from a blend of white wines. The wine is fermented, aged, and filtered to produce a vinegar with a slightly lower acidity level than red wine vinegar.

Ready-to-Use Broths

Ready-made, gluten-free vegetable broth is used for a selection of savory recipes in this collection. Opt for certified organic broths that are gluten-free, reduced sodium, and MSG-free. For convenience, look for broths in Tetra Paks, which typically come in 32-ounce, 48-ounce, and occasionally 16-ounce sizes. Once opened, these can be stored in the refrigerator for up to 1 week.

Measuring Ingredients

Accurate measurement of chickpea flour (see page 16) is critical for the success of all of the recipes in this collection. Measuring the remaining ingredients in a given recipe demands the same care. Here are my tips for precise measurement:

Measuring Dry Ingredients

With the exception of measuring chickpea flour, dry ingredients in this collection, such as leavening agents (e.g., baking powder or baking soda), spices, or cocoa powder, should be measured in the following manner: Lightly spoon or scoop the ingredient into the appropriate-size dry measuring cup or measuring spoon, heaping it up over the top. Next, slide a straight-edged utensil, such as a knife, across the top to level off the extra. Avoid shaking or tapping the cup or spoon, or tamping down on the ingredient with another utensil, to settle or level off the ingredient; doing so will result in a greater quantity than you need.

Measuring Moist Ingredients

Moist ingredients, such as brown sugar, coconut, and dried fruit, are also measured in dry measuring cups and measuring spoons. Fill the appropriate-size measuring cup or spoon to slightly overflowing, then pack down the ingredient firmly with the back of a spoon. Add more of the ingredient and pack down again until the cup is full and even with the top of the measure.

Measuring Liquid Ingredients

All liquid ingredients should be measured with a clear plastic or glass measuring cup or container with measurement lines that are clearly marked up the sides of the container. Place the container on the counter and lower your head to read the measurement at eye level (looking down at the container will distort the measurement lines). Pour the liquid ingredient to the appropriate mark.

breakfast

fresh herb chickpea scramble 37

loaded southwestern chickpea omelet 38

new classic buttermilk pancakes 40

cottage cheese pancakes
with blueberry chia jam 41

pumpkin spice waffles 42

parisian crêpes 43

dutch baby puffed pancake 44

old-fashioned waffles 47

newfangled applesauce raisin muffins 48

cranberry tangerine muffins 49

bakery-style blueberry muffins 50

cinnamon apple fritter puffs 52

ginger scones with
chickpea lemon curd 53

raspberry coconut mini clafoutis 57

fresh herb chickpea scramble

That's right: you can scramble chickpeas! Simply mix chickpea flour, water, salt, and a pinch of turmeric for golden color, and you have the makings of some great scrambled "eggs" without ever breaking a shell. I'm partial to chopped shallots and fresh herbs in my scramble, but just like the egg variety, you can make this your own with the ingredients and seasonings you prefer. **MAKES 2 SERVINGS**

¾ cup water
⅔ cup (80 grams) chickpea flour
½ teaspoon ground turmeric

¼ teaspoon fine sea salt
1 tablespoon olive oil
⅓ cup minced shallots
1 tablespoon chopped fresh, flat-leaf parsley leaves

1 tablespoon chopped fresh basil
Freshly ground black pepper

1. In a small bowl, whisk the water, flour, turmeric, and salt until smooth. Let stand for at least 10 minutes or for up to 1 hour.

2. In a medium skillet, heat the olive oil over medium heat. Add the shallots; cook, stirring, for 4 to 5 minutes, until softened but not browned.

3. Pour the chickpea batter into the skillet; let it cook, without touching it, for 3 to 5 minutes, until the edges begin to set. Using a spatula, break up the mixture to resemble scramble eggs. Add the parsley and basil; continue to cook, stirring, until the scramble appears set (i.e., no wet batter).

4. Season to taste with pepper and serve immediately.

tip
The turmeric gives the scramble the yellow color of scrambled eggs. You can skip it if you do not have any.

VARIATIONS

Cherry Tomato Scramble: Omit the parsley. Replace the shallots with 1 cup cherry tomatoes, halved.

Spicy Kale Scramble: Omit the parsley and basil. Add ¼ teaspoon red pepper flakes and 1 cup packed chopped kale leaves (tough stems removed) along with the shallots; increase total cooking time for the vegetables to 5 to 7 minutes.

Roasted Pepper and Basil Scramble: Omit the parsley and double the amount of basil. Replace the shallots with ½ cup chopped roasted red bell peppers (from a jar, drained). Decrease the cooking time in step two to 1 minute.

loaded southwestern chickpea omelet

Few things can beat an omelet when you're hankering for a savory breakfast, and this egg-free chickpea flour omelet is no exception. Here, a Southwestern blend of vegetables and toppings gives the essential omelet extra panache, but your take can be as simple or complex as you like. **MAKES 1 SERVING**

¼ cup (30 grams) chickpea flour

1 tablespoon grated Parmesan cheese

2 teaspoons flaxseed meal (ground flaxseeds)

¼ teaspoon baking powder

¼ teaspoon ground turmeric

⅛ teaspoon fine sea salt

6 tablespoons water

4 teaspoons olive oil

¾ cup sliced mushrooms

⅓ cup chopped red bell pepper

¼ cup chopped green onions

½ teaspoon ground cumin

SUGGESTED ACCOMPANIMENTS

Prepared salsa

Mashed avocado or guacamole

Chopped fresh cilantro

Lime wedges

1. Whisk together the flour, Parmesan, flaxseed meal, baking powder, turmeric, and salt in a small bowl until blended. Add the water; whisk until blended and smooth. Let stand at room temperature for at least 10 minutes or up to 1 hour.

2. Heat 2 teaspoons of the olive oil in a small skillet set over medium-high heat. Add the mushrooms and peppers; cook, stirring, for 5 minutes. Add the green onions and cumin; cook, stirring, for 2 minutes longer. Transfer the vegetables to a small plate. Wipe out the skillet.

3. Reduce the heat to medium; heat the remaining 2 teaspoons olive oil in same skillet. Pour the omelet batter into the pan, tilting the pan so that the batter is evenly spread. Cover with a tight-fitting lid and cook for 4 minutes, until the top appears somewhat dry.

4. Add the vegetables to one side of the omelet and fold the other half over it. Cover and cook for another 3 to 4 minutes. Serve with any of the suggested accompaniments.

make it vegan!
Use an equal amount of nutritional yeast flakes in place of the Parmesan cheese, or simply omit.

Asparagus and Chive Omelet: Prepare the omelet batter as directed, adding 1 tablespoon minced chives and ¼ teaspoon dried thyme leaves. For the filling, cook ¾ cup diced (¼-inch pieces) asparagus in place of the mushroom-pepper filling. Omit the toppings.

Zucchini Omelet: Prepare the omelet batter as directed, adding ¼ teaspoon dried marjoram. For the filling, cook 1½ cups shredded zucchini in place of the mushroom-pepper filling. Add ½ cup shredded Gruyere cheese to the omelet along with the cooked zucchini. Omit the toppings.

Cauliflower Feta Omelet: Prepare the omelet batter as directed. For the filling, cook 1¼ cups chopped cauliflower in place of the mushroom-pepper filling. Add ⅓ cup crumbled feta cheese to the omelet along with the cooked cauliflower. Omit the toppings.

new classic buttermilk pancakes

Whether it's an early weekday morning, a lazy Sunday, or a few hours past midnight, sometimes all you want is a stack of fluffy buttermilk pancakes. My chickpea flour rendition is sure to hit the spot. **MAKES ABOUT 18 (3-INCH) PANCAKES**

2 cups (240 grams) chickpea flour
1¾ teaspoons baking soda
¾ teaspoon fine sea salt
2 large eggs

1⅔ cups buttermilk
1 tablespoon fresh lemon juice
1½ tablespoons natural cane sugar
½ teaspoon vanilla extract

Cooking spray or vegetable oil, for cooking
Pure maple syrup, for serving

1. Preheat the oven to 250°F.

2. In a large bowl, whisk together the flour, baking soda, and salt.

3. In a medium bowl, whisk the eggs; whisk in the buttermilk, lemon juice, sugar, and vanilla. Add to the flour mixture, whisking until just blended.

4. Heat a large nonstick griddle or skillet over medium heat. Spray it with cooking spray or brush with vegetable oil. For each pancake, pour about ¼ cup batter onto the griddle. Cook the pancakes until bubbles appear on top. Turn each pancake over and cook for about 1 minute, until golden brown. Transfer to a heatproof plate and keep warm, covered, in the oven.

5. Repeat with the remaining batter, spraying the griddle and adjusting the heat as necessary between batches. Serve with maple syrup.

make it vegan!
Replace the eggs with 2 psyllium "eggs" (page 18), and replace the buttermilk with nondairy buttermilk (page 21).

VARIATIONS

Maple Chocolate Chip Pancakes: Replace the sugar with an equal amount of pure maple syrup and increase the vanilla to 1 teaspoon. Sprinkle 1½ teaspoons miniature semisweet chocolate chips onto each pancake before flipping.

Lemon Poppy Seed Pancakes: Omit the vanilla; add 2 teaspoons finely grated lemon zest and 1 tablespoon poppy seeds to the batter. Serve with fresh fruit and honey, if desired.

Blueberry Pancakes: Sprinkle 4 to 6 (depending on size) blueberries onto each pancake before flipping.

cottage cheese pancakes with blueberry chia jam

If cheesecake is your idea of the perfect breakfast, then meet your new favorite pancakes. Regardless of your feelings toward cottage cheese, I can assure you that mixing it into pancake batter results in a light, cheesecake-y, blintz-like stack of deliciousness that is made even more delectable with a no-cook blueberry and chia jam. **MAKES 16 PANCAKES**

CHIA JAM
1½ cups fresh or frozen (thawed) blueberries
1½ tablespoons chia seeds
1 tablespoon pure maple syrup

PANCAKES
¾ cup (90 grams) chickpea flour
1 teaspoon baking powder
¼ teaspoon fine sea salt
4 large eggs
1½ cups cottage cheese

½ cup milk
2 tablespoons pure maple syrup
1 teaspoon vanilla extract
Cooking spray or vegetable oil, for cooking

1. To make the jam, process the blueberries, chia seeds, and maple syrup in a food processor until smooth. Transfer to a small bowl; refrigerate until ready to serve.

2. To make the pancakes, whisk together the flour, baking powder, and salt in a small bowl.

3. In a medium bowl, whisk together the eggs, cottage cheese, milk, maple syrup, and vanilla until blended.

4. Add the flour mixture to the cottage cheese mixture and stir until just blended.

5. Heat a large nonstick griddle or skillet over medium heat. Spray with cooking spray or brush with vegetable oil. For each pancake, pour about ¼ cup batter onto the griddle. Cook until bubbles appear on top. Flip the pancakes and cook for about 1 minute, until golden brown. Repeat with the remaining batter, spraying the griddle and adjusting the heat as necessary between batches.

6. Serve the pancakes topped with chia jam.

tips

An equal amount of other fruits and berries, such as raspberries, mangoes, blackberries, or kiwi can be used in place of the blueberries.

Feel free to use an equal amount of other sweeteners, too, such as honey, natural cane sugar, or coconut palm sugar.

pumpkin spice waffles

It takes only one forkful of these waffles to make it clear why just about everyone loves pumpkin and spice. But don't take my word for it: make a batch, pronto, and don't you dare wait until autumn to do so. MAKES ABOUT 6 WAFFLES

1¼ cups (150 grams) chickpea flour

2½ teaspoons pumpkin pie spice

2¼ teaspoons baking powder

1 teaspoon baking soda

½ teaspoon fine sea salt

2 large eggs

¾ cup buttermilk

¾ cup pumpkin purée (not pie filling)

3 tablespoons unsalted butter, melted and cooled

3 tablespoons coconut palm sugar or packed light brown sugar

1 teaspoon vanilla extract

Vegetable oil, for cooking

Pure maple syrup, for serving

1. Preheat the oven to 250°F and preheat a waffle iron to medium heat.

2. In a large bowl, whisk together the flour, pumpkin pie spice, baking powder, baking soda, and salt.

3. In a medium bowl, whisk the eggs; whisk in the buttermilk, pumpkin, melted butter, coconut sugar, and vanilla. Add this to the flour mixture, whisking until just blended.

4. Generously brush the waffle iron with vegetable oil. Ladle about ½ cup batter into the waffle mold. Cook the waffles according to manufacturer's instructions until golden and cooked through, 1½ to 2 minutes. Give the waffle iron one hard press before opening (this helps to prevent the waffle from separating when you open the iron).

5. Transfer the finished waffles directly onto a rack in the oven to stay warm, keeping them in a single layer to maintain crispness. Repeat with the remaining batter.

6. Serve with maple syrup.

VARIATION

Pumpkin-Cranberry Waffles: Prepare as directed, but add ¾ cup packed dried cranberries, finely chopped, to the batter before using.

make it vegan!

Replace the eggs with 2 psyllium "eggs" (page 18), replace the butter with melted virgin coconut oil or neutral vegetable oil, and replace the buttermilk with nondairy buttermilk (page 21).

parisian crêpes

Crêpes epitomize the appeal of minimalism: simple ingredients, no fancy-pants prep, and almost foolproof results. Chickpea flour produces especially tender crêpes that can be taken in any sweet or savory direction you choose. Additionally, you can use the crêpes as tortillas, sandwich wrappers, or as a gluten-free, grain-free noodle replacement in lasagna. **MAKES 7 TO 8 MEDIUM-LARGE CRÊPES**

⅔ cup (80 grams)
  chickpea flour
¼ teaspoon fine sea salt

2 large eggs
⅔ cup milk

2 tablespoons olive oil
Nonstick cooking spray

1. In a blender or food processor, process the flour, salt, eggs, milk, and olive oil until smooth. Cover and refrigerate for 30 minutes.

2. Heat a large nonstick skillet over medium-high heat. Remove the pan from the heat and lightly spray it with cooking spray. Whisk the crêpe batter slightly.

3. Pour about ¼ cup batter into the pan, quickly tilting in all directions to cover the bottom of the pan. Cook for about 45 seconds, until just golden at the edges. With a spatula, carefully lift an edge of the crêpe to test for doneness; it should be golden brown on the bottom and able to be shaken loose from the pan. Turn the crêpe over and cook for 15 to 30 seconds, until golden brown.

4. Transfer the crêpe to a clean kitchen towel to cool completely. Repeat with the remaining batter, spraying the skillet and adjusting the heat as necessary between batches, stacking cooled crêpes between sheets of waxed paper to prevent sticking.

5. Fill each crêpe with a filling of your choice and fold in half, into quarters, or roll up.

make it vegan!
Replace the eggs with 2 psyllium "eggs" (page 18) and replace the milk with nondairy milk.

storage tip
Refrigerate the crêpes, stacked between sheets of waxed paper and tightly covered in plastic wrap, for up to 2 days or freeze, enclosed in a resealable plastic bag, for up to 1 month.

FILLING SUGGESTIONS

- Lemon juice and a drizzle of honey or a sprinkle of natural cane sugar
- Tahini or yogurt and fresh fruit or jam.
- Grated bittersweet chocolate
- Sautéed greens (e.g., kale or spinach) and grated Parmesan cheese (or a sprinkle of nutritional yeast flakes).
- Sautéed thinly sliced apples and a drizzle of pure maple syrup.

dutch baby puffed pancake

I don't scream over pancakes (very often), but that's exactly what I did when I opened the oven door upon my very first rendition of this recipe. Gloriously golden brown and puffed to heavenly heights, it looked exactly like the Dutch baby pancakes my mother made throughout my childhood (only more gorgeous). I would have screamed again when I tasted it, but my mouth was too stuffed with lemon-sugary, buttery deliciousness. **MAKES 4 SERVINGS**

---

3 large eggs
¾ cup milk
⅔ cup (80 grams) chickpea flour

¼ teaspoon fine sea salt
3 tablespoons unsalted butter

2 tablespoons natural cane sugar
1½ tablespoons fresh lemon juice

1. Place a 9- or 10-inch cast iron skillet or other oven-proof skillet in the oven. Preheat the oven to 450°F.

2. Place the eggs and milk in a blender or food processor; process until blended. Add the flour and salt; process until completely blended and smooth, scraping the sides as needed.

3. Remove the skillet from the oven (be careful; it will be extremely hot). Add the butter and melt, swirling to coat. Add all of the batter and immediately return the skillet to the oven.

4. Bake for 15 to 20 minutes, until puffed and golden brown. Cut into 4 equal wedges and serve sprinkled with sugar and lemon juice.

tips

An equal amount of olive oil or virgin coconut oil can be used in place of the butter.

An equal amount of nondairy milk can be used in place of the dairy milk.

A 9-inch round or square cake pan (metal or glass) can be used in place of the cast iron skillet. Preheat the pan in the same manner as the skillet.

Browned Butter Raspberry Muffins: Melt the butter in a medium saucepan over medium heat and cook for 3 to 5 minutes, stirring often, until it foams, then browns. Cool completely and use in the recipe as directed. Replace the blueberries with an equal amount of raspberries.

Lemon Blueberry Muffins: Reduce the amount of vanilla to 1 teaspoon. Add 1 tablespoon finely grated lemon zest along with the vanilla.

storage tip

Store the cooled muffins in an airtight container in the refrigerator for up to 3 days or in the freezer for up to 3 months. Let thaw at room temperature for 1 to 2 hours before serving.

cinnamon apple fritter puffs

With little nuggets of apple and enhanced with cinnamon and maple syrup, these newfangled fritters are a far cry from the greasy, sugar-bomb versions at the doughnut shop. I confess, they are equally addictive, but since they are made with the kind of fuel you need to start your day—fiber, protein, and fresh fruit—you can feel virtuous eating an extra one. Or two. Or, perhaps, three. **MAKES 20 FRITTERS**

1¼ cups (150 grams) chickpea flour
1 teaspoon ground cinnamon
½ teaspoon baking soda
¼ teaspoon fine sea salt

½ cup unsweetened apple juice
2 tablespoons pure maple syrup
1 tablespoon fresh lemon juice

1½ cups chopped peeled tart-sweet apple
2 tablespoons neutral vegetable oil
Natural cane sugar (optional)

1. In a medium bowl, whisk together the flour, cinnamon, baking soda, and salt until blended. Add the apple juice, maple syrup, and lemon juice, whisking until blended. Let stand at room temperature for 10 minutes; stir in the apples.

2. Heat the oil in a large skillet set over medium-high heat.

3. Scoop the batter in 2-tablespoon-size portions into the skillet, flattening with the back of a spoon. Cook for about 2 minutes per side, until golden brown and puffed up. Transfer to a paper towel-lined plate to drain.

4. Sprinkle the fritters with sugar. Serve warm.

tip
For the apples, consider using Gala, Braeburn, or Golden Delicious.

VARIATIONS

Baked Apple Fritter Puffs: Place a greased baking sheet in a preheated, 400°F oven for 12 minutes. Remove the sheet and scoop the batter in 2-tablespoon-size portions onto it, flattening with the back of a spoon. Bake for 15 minutes. Brush with 1 tablespoon vegetable oil, then flip. Bake for 12 to 15 minutes longer, until golden brown and crispy. Sprinkle with sugar.

Tart Cherry Fritters: Soak 1 cup dried tart cherries in hot (not boiling) water for 10 minutes; drain, pat dry, and coarsely chop. Use in place of the apples and replace the cinnamon with ¾ teaspoon ground cardamom.

Spiced Pear Fritters: Replace the apple with an equal amount of diced, peeled, firm-ripe pear, the maple syrup with honey, and the cinnamon with ½ teaspoon ground nutmeg.

ginger scones with chickpea lemon curd

These tender scones double your ginger pleasure with hits from both ground and candied ginger. As for the lemon curd: making it is a command, not a suggestion. Prepare to be wowed! **MAKES 8 SCONES**

2 cups (240 grams) chickpea flour, plus more for dusting

8 tablespoons natural cane sugar

1 tablespoon ground ginger

2 teaspoons baking powder

¼ teaspoon baking soda

¼ teaspoon fine sea salt

5 tablespoons cold unsalted butter, cut into small cubes

½ cup chopped candied (crystallized) ginger (optional)

½ cup plain yogurt

1 teaspoon vanilla extract

Chickpea Lemon Curd (recipe follows)

1. Preheat the oven to 350°F. Line a large rimmed baking sheet with parchment paper.

2. In a large bowl, whisk together the flour, 7 tablespoons of the sugar, the ground ginger, baking powder, baking soda, and salt. Using your fingers or a pastry cutter, work the butter into the flour mixture until the dough is crumbly and resembles fresh breadcrumbs. Stir in the candied ginger.

3. In a small bowl, whisk together the yogurt and vanilla until blended and add to the flour mixture. Stir until just blended.

4. Turn the dough out onto a lightly floured clean work surface and knead briefly until it comes together. Gently pat it into a 6-inch square about ¾ inch thick. Cut into four 3-inch squares; cut each square in half on the diagonal. Place the triangles 2 inches apart on the prepared baking sheet. Sprinkle with the remaining tablespoon of sugar.

5. Bake for 13 to 18 minutes, until golden brown. Transfer the scones to a wire rack and cool slightly or completely. Serve with the lemon curd.

VARIATION

Teatime Currant Scones: Omit the ground ginger and replace the candied ginger with ½ cup dried currants (or coarsely chopped raisins).

make it vegan!
Use cold virgin coconut oil in place of the butter and plain nondairy yogurt in place of the yogurt.

storage tip
Store the cooled scones in an airtight container in the refrigerator for up to 2 days or in the freezer for up to 3 months. Let thaw at room temperature for 1 to 2 hours before serving.

Chickpea Lemon Curd

I considered using *magical* in the title of this recipe. How else to explain the transformation of beans into lemon curd? And not just any lemon curd, but a silken, tart-sweet treat that you'd swear is loaded with egg yolks. MAKES ABOUT 1 CUP

⅔ cup natural cane sugar
2 teaspoons finely grated lemon zest
⅔ cup fresh lemon juice
¼ cup (30 grams) chickpea flour
¾ cup water
⅛ teaspoon fine sea salt
4 tablespoons unsalted butter, cut into pieces

1. In a medium saucepan, whisk the sugar, lemon zest, lemon juice, flour, water, and salt until smooth. Cook over medium heat, whisking constantly, for 8 to 10 minutes, until it's thick and creamy. Add the butter, whisking until blended and smooth.

2. Transfer the curd to a small, heatproof bowl or container; cool completely. Press a piece of waxed paper or plastic wrap against the surface of the curd and refrigerate until cold.

make it vegan!
Use an equal amount of virgin coconut oil in place of the butter.

storage tip
Store in an airtight container in the refrigerator for up to 2 weeks. If the curd separates after a few days, process in a food processor for 1 minute (or whisk vigorously by hand) to bring it back together.

raspberry coconut mini clafoutis

Clafoutis—a traditional French fruit dessert that's part custard, part pancake—finds new expression as a make-and-go breakfast. A honey-sweetened batter of chickpea flour and coconut milk stands in for the traditional egg, milk, and sugar custard, making the assembly extra simple. **MAKES 12 MINI CLAFOUTIS**

Nonstick cooking spray
2⅓ cups (280 grams) chickpea flour
1½ cups well-stirred full-fat coconut milk

1¼ cups warm (not hot) water
⅓ cup honey
1 teaspoon vanilla extract

1 teaspoon fine sea salt
1½ cups fresh raspberries

1. Preheat the oven to 500°F. Spray the cups of a 12-count standard muffin tin with nonstick cooking spray.

2. In a large bowl, whisk the flour, coconut milk, water, honey, vanilla, and salt until blended and smooth.

3. Divide the raspberries evenly among the prepared cups; ladle the batter evenly over the raspberries in the cups.

4. Bake for 12 minutes. Crack open the oven door to release steam; close the door and bake for 10 to 15 minutes longer, until golden brown. Transfer to a wire rack and cool for 15 minutes. Carefully remove from tin. Serve warm or cool completely.

VARIATION

You can use other fruits and berries such as blueberries, diced peaches, or cherries in place of the raspberries. Alternatively, use 1 cup dried fruit (e.g., diced dried apricots, raisins, or tart cherries), soaked in hot water for 10 minutes before using, then drained.

make it vegan!
Use an equal amount of pure maple syrup in place of the honey.

storage tip
Store the cooled clafoutis in an airtight container in the refrigerator for up to 1 week. Alternatively, store in an airtight container and freeze for up to 1 month. Let the frozen clafoutis thaw at room temperature for about 1 hour or microwave on high for 1 to 2 minutes.

breads

farinata
(la farina genovese)

Farinata is a chickpea flour flatbread that, along with basil pesto, is one of the iconic dishes of Liguria, the coastal region of northwestern Italy. The recipe is as simple as mixing flour, water, salt, and pepper, and then baking to perfection in a bit of sizzling olive oil. The only catch: you need to let the batter rest for at least three hours, or up to twenty-four hours, to produce the best flavor (mildly nutty) and texture (creamy near the middle, crispy at the edges). Farinata is terrific as a stand-alone bread or as a base for, well, just about any topping you like. Alternatively, you can also make slightly thinner pancakes known as socca. Socca is a specialty of Nice, France, which happens to be a mere thirty miles from the border of Liguria. **MAKES 6 SERVINGS**

2 cups (240 grams) chickpea flour

1 teaspoon fine sea salt

Pinch of freshly ground black pepper

3 cups warm (not hot) water

5 tablespoons olive oil

1. In a large bowl, whisk together the flour, salt, and pepper. Whisk in the water and 3 tablespoons of the olive oil until well blended and smooth. Cover the bowl with a clean kitchen towel and let stand at room temperature for at least 3 hours or for up to 24 hours.

2. Preheat the oven to 500°F. Pour 1 tablespoon of the remaining oil in a 9-inch cast iron skillet (or other ovenproof skillet); heat in the oven for 10 minutes.

3. Remove the skillet from the oven; pour in half of the batter, swirling to coat. Bake for 12 minutes; crack open the oven door to release steam. Close the oven door and bake for 6 to 8 minutes longer, until golden brown and crispy at the edges. Use a metal spatula to release the farinata, and transfer it to a plate.

4. Repeat with the remaining oil and batter. Cut each farinata into 6 wedges. Serve warm or at room temperature.

Irish Brown Bread: Omit the topping. Replace the honey with dark cooking molasses (not blackstrap) and replace the olive oil with an equal amount of unsalted butter, melted.

Caraway Currant Soda Bread: Omit the topping. Add ½ cup currants and 1 tablespoon caraway seeds, coarsely crushed, to the buttermilk mixture.

Sesame Soda Bread: Omit the topping. Add 1 tablespoon toasted sesame seeds to the buttermilk mixture.

Golden Raisin Soda Bread: Omit the topping. Add ½ cup golden raisins and 2 teaspoons finely grated orange zest to the buttermilk mixture.

storage tip

Store the cooled breads, wrapped in foil or plastic wrap, in the refrigerator for up to 1 week. Alternatively, individually wrap each bread in plastic wrap, then foil, completely enclosing the breads, and freeze for up to 3 months. Let thaw at room temperature for 4 to 6 hours before serving.

chickpea no-corn bread

This is an example of a recipe that began life as something entirely different. I was experimenting (unsuccessfully) with several savory chickpea flour bread ideas when my son entered the kitchen, asking if he could have a piece of the "cornbread" cooling on the counter. Rather than correct him, I cut a square and handed it over. An enthusiastic "Yum!" quickly followed; he even asked for "more of that cornbread" for dinner. He was right: the bread looked, smelled, and tasted like (a darn good!) cornbread. It only took a few more tweaks (a bit of pumpkin for texture and color, a hint of cumin and honey for flavor) to make this no-corn cornbread spot-on. **MAKES 12 SERVINGS**

Nonstick cooking spray
1½ cups (180 grams) chickpea flour
2½ teaspoons baking powder

½ teaspoon ground cumin
½ teaspoon fine sea salt
2 large eggs
¾ cup milk

⅓ cup olive oil
⅓ cup pumpkin purée (not pie filling)
1 tablespoon honey

1. Preheat the oven to 350°F. Line an 8-inch square baking pan with parchment paper, leaving a 2-inch overhang on two opposing sides. Spray the paper and exposed sides of the pan with nonstick cooking spray.

2. In a large bowl, whisk together the flour, baking powder, cumin, and salt.

3. In a medium bowl, combine the eggs, milk, oil, pumpkin, and honey until well blended.

4. Add the pumpkin mixture to the flour mixture and stir until just blended. Spread the batter evenly in the prepared pan.

5. Bake for 23 to 28 minutes, until the edges are golden brown and a toothpick inserted in the center comes out clean. Let the bread cool in the pan on a wire rack for 10 minutes. Hold on to the paper overhang to transfer it directly to the rack to cool completely. Remove the paper and cut the bread into 12 pieces to serve.

make it vegan!
Replace the eggs with 2 psyllium "eggs" (page 18), replace the milk with nondairy milk, and replace the honey with pure maple syrup.

VARIATIONS

Green Onion No-Corn Bread: Add 1¼ cups chopped green onions to the batter.

Chipotle-Roasted Red Pepper Bread: Add 1 teaspoon chipotle chile powder along with the cumin. Add 1 cup chopped roasted red bell peppers (from a jar, drained) to the finished batter before spreading it in the baking pan.

super-seed supper muffins

Flax and chia seeds have received much attention in recent years for their myriad health benefits. While the two seeds are worthy of the praise, good old-fashioned, familiar, inexpensive sunflower seeds are also pretty special. In addition to being rich in polyunsaturated fats, plant sterols, and minerals, they are also very high in vitamin E, a powerful antioxidant. But all you need to know here is that all three seeds add terrific flavor and crunch to these savory, go-with-anything muffins. **MAKES 16 MUFFINS**

Nonstick cooking spray
1⅓ cups (160 grams) chickpea flour
⅔ cup flaxseed meal (ground flaxseeds)

1 teaspoon baking soda
½ teaspoon fine sea salt
2 large eggs
1½ cups plain yogurt
½ cup olive oil

1 tablespoon honey
½ cup toasted sunflower seeds, chopped
¼ cup chia seeds

1. Preheat the oven to 350°F. Spray 16 cups of two 12-count standard muffin tins with nonstick cooking spray.

2. In a large bowl, whisk together the flour, flaxseed meal, baking soda, and salt.

3. In a medium bowl, whisk together the eggs, yogurt, oil, and honey until well blended; add this to the flour mixture along with the sunflower and chia seeds, stirring until just blended. Divide the batter equally among the prepared muffin cups.

4. Bake for 15 to 20 minutes, until a toothpick inserted in the center comes out clean. Let the muffins cool in the pan on a wire rack for 5 minutes, then release to the rack to cool.

make it vegan!
Replace the yogurt with nondairy yogurt, replace the eggs with 2 psyllium "eggs" (page 18), and replace the honey with pure maple syrup.

storage tip
Store the cooled muffins in an airtight container in the refrigerator for up to 5 days or in the freezer for up to 3 months. Let thaw at room temperature for 1 to 2 hours before serving.

chickpea beer bread

My mother is an excellent yeast bread baker, but when I was little, she relied heavily on an arsenal of quick bread recipes—both sweet and savory—to supplement or star at mealtimes. Beer bread appeared often, especially on soup nights. The preparation could not be easier, but the result is a yeasty (thanks to the beer) loaf that tastes like a multi-step, many-hour creation. Here, the nutty flavor of chickpea flour deepens the malty flavors of the beer to extra-delicious effect. **MAKES 1 LOAF**

Nonstick cooking spray
2½ cups (300 grams) chickpea flour
2 tablespoons natural cane sugar

1 tablespoon baking powder
1½ teaspoons baking soda

¾ teaspoon fine sea salt
1 (12-ounce) bottle beer (gluten-free)

1. Preheat the oven to 350°F. Spray a 9 by 5-inch loaf pan with nonstick cooking spray.

2. In a large bowl, whisk together the flour, sugar, baking powder, baking soda, and salt.

3. Add the beer to the flour mixture and stir until just blended. Spread the batter evenly in the prepared pan.

4. Bake for 43 to 48 minutes, until a toothpick inserted in the center comes out clean. Let the bread cool in the pan on a wire rack for 10 minutes, then release to the rack to cool.

VARIATIONS

Molasses Stout Bread: Replace the sugar with an equal amount of dark (not blackstrap) molasses. Use a gluten-free stout for the beer.

Dilled Beer Bread: Add 1 tablespoon minced fresh dill or 1½ teaspoons dried dill to the batter.

Sharp Cheddar Beer Bread: Add 1½ cups shredded sharp Cheddar cheese to the batter.

Fresh Herb Beer Bread: Add ½ cup loosely packed flat-leaf parsley leaves, chopped; ¼ cup packed basil leaves, chopped; and 2 tablespoons minced chives to the batter.

tips
Do not open the beer until you are ready to mix the batter to avoid any loss of carbonation—the bubbles help to give this yeasty bread its light and airy rise.

An equal amount of coconut sugar or packed light brown sugar can be used in place of the natural cane sugar.

storage tip
Store the cooled bread, wrapped in foil or plastic wrap, in the refrigerator for up to 5 days. Alternatively, wrap it in plastic wrap, then foil, completely enclosing the bread, and freeze for up to 3 months. Let thaw at room temperature for 4 to 6 hours before serving.

sundried tomato & spinach bread

A piece of bread that comes fully loaded with vegetables and cheese is my idea of a great lunch. Or snack. Or breakfast. The combination of sundried tomatoes, spinach, and feta is especially satisfying when the bread batter is made with high-protein chickpea flour. **MAKES 16 SERVINGS**

Nonstick cooking spray
1¾ cups (210 grams) chickpea flour
1 tablespoon baking powder
1½ teaspoons dried basil
½ teaspoon baking soda

¾ teaspoon fine sea salt
2 large eggs
¾ cup milk
¼ cup olive oil
2 teaspoons natural cane sugar

1 (10-ounce) package frozen chopped spinach, thawed and squeezed dry
½ cup chopped, drained, oil-packed sun-dried tomatoes
½ cup crumbled feta cheese (optional)

1. Preheat the oven to 350°F. Line a 9-inch square baking pan with parchment paper, leaving a 2-inch overhang on two opposing sides. Spray the paper and exposed sides of the pan with nonstick cooking spray.

2. In a large bowl, whisk together the flour, baking powder, basil, baking soda, and salt.

3. In a medium bowl, combine the eggs, milk, oil, and sugar until well blended.

4. Add the egg mixture to the flour mixture and stir until just blended. Stir in the spinach, tomatoes, and feta. Spread the batter evenly in the prepared pan.

5. Bake for 23 to 28 minutes, until the edges are golden brown and a toothpick inserted in the center comes out clean. Let the bread cool in the pan on a wire rack for 10 minutes. Hold on to the paper overhang to transfer it directly onto the rack to cool completely. Remove the paper and cut the bread into 16 pieces.

make it vegan!
Replace the eggs with 2 psyllium "eggs" (page 18) and replace the milk with nondairy milk. Omit the feta cheese and add ¼ cup nutritional yeast flakes (if desired).

VARIATION

Spinach-Artichoke Bread: Omit the basil and add 2 cloves garlic, minced. Replace the tomatoes with ⅔ cup chopped, drained marinated artichoke hearts. Replace the feta cheese with an equal amount of freshly grated Parmesan cheese (or ⅓ cup nutritional yeast flakes for vegan option).

pudla (spicy indian chickpea crêpes)

Doubly spicy thanks to the jalapeño and ginger, these Indian crêpes made all of my taste-testers swoon. Make them a bit smaller (and slightly thicker) than other crêpes and use them in place of utensils the next time you make your favorite curry, or make them full-size and use as a wrap with your favorite sandwich fixings. **MAKES 10 PUDLAS**

1⅓ cups (160 grams) chickpea flour
1 cup water
2 teaspoons minced jalapeño chile

1 cup loosely packed fresh cilantro leaves
1½ tablespoons peeled, minced fresh ginger
1 teaspoon fine sea salt

½ teaspoon chili powder
Nonstick cooking spray

1. In a blender or food processor, process the flour, water, jalapeño, cilantro, ginger, salt, and chili powder until blended and smooth. Cover and let stand at room temperature for at least 2 hours.

2. Heat a large nonstick skillet over medium-high heat. Remove from heat and lightly spray the pan with cooking spray. Whisk the batter slightly.

3. Pour about ¼ cup batter into the pan, quickly tilting it in all directions to cover the bottom of the pan (the crêpe will be fairly thin). Cook for about 30 seconds, until just golden at the edges. With a spatula, carefully lift an edge of the pudla to test for doneness; it is ready to turn when it is golden brown on the bottom and can be shaken loose from the pan. Flip the pudla and cook for 15 to 30 seconds, until golden brown.

4. Transfer the pudla to a plate. Repeat with the remaining batter, spraying the skillet and adjusting the heat as necessary between batches, stacking the cooled pudla between sheets of waxed paper to prevent sticking.

storage tip
Refrigerate the pudla between sheets of waxed paper, tightly covered in plastic wrap, for up to 2 days or freeze, enclosed in a resealable plastic bag, for up to 1 month.

VARIATION

Plain Indian Pudla: Omit the jalapeño, cilantro, ginger, and chili powder.

cheddar, chive & chickpea buttermilk biscuits

I think you could convince me to try just about any food or flavor combination so long as you piled it on a buttermilk biscuit. These chickpea flour biscuits are no exception to the rule. Rather, they just rule. If you want to make the cheese really pop (both in the literal and figurative sense), dice it rather than shred it. The cheese will explode from the sides of the biscuits in blissful blobs ranging from gooey to crispy.

MAKES 12 BISCUITS

2¼ cups (270 grams) chickpea flour

2 teaspoons natural cane sugar

1 tablespoon baking powder

¾ teaspoon baking soda

¾ teaspoon salt

7 tablespoons cold unsalted butter, cut into small pieces

1 cup buttermilk

1½ cups shredded sharp Cheddar cheese

⅓ cup chopped chives

1. Preheat the oven to 400°F. Line a large baking sheet with parchment paper.

2. In a large bowl, whisk together the flour, sugar, baking powder, baking soda, and salt. Using a pastry cutter or your fingers, work the butter into the flour mixture until the dough is crumbly. Add the buttermilk and stir until just blended; fold in the cheese and chives.

3. Drop the dough in 12 equal mounds onto the prepared baking sheet, spacing them 2 inches apart.

4. Bake for 10 to 13 minutes, until golden brown on top. Cool slightly. Serve warm.

tip
The chives can be replaced with ½ cup chopped green onions.

make it vegan!
Replace the butter with chilled nonhydrogenated organic vegetable shortening and replace the buttermilk with nondairy buttermilk (page 21). Omit the cheese or use an equal amount of nondairy Cheddar cheese.

VARIATIONS

Buttermilk Biscuits: Omit the cheese and chives.

Toasted Coconut Biscuits: Replace the butter with chilled virgin coconut oil and increase the sugar to 1 tablespoon. Replace the cheese and chives with 1¼ cups toasted, unsweetened flaked coconut.

brown sugar banana bread

It turns out that chickpea flour and bananas have a natural affinity for each other, a relationship strengthened all the more by a bit of brown sugar. I use baking powder instead of baking soda for leavening; the latter produces a squidgy banana bread while the former renders the lighter, cakelike loaf I prefer. **MAKES 1 LOAF**

Nonstick cooking spray
1½ cups (180 grams) chickpea flour
1 tablespoon baking powder

1 teaspoon ground cinnamon
½ teaspoon fine sea salt
2 large eggs
1⅓ cups mashed very ripe bananas (about 3 large bananas)

½ cup packed light brown sugar
5 tablespoons unsalted butter, melted and cooled
2 teaspoons vanilla extract

1. Preheat the oven to 350°F. Line a 9 by 5-inch loaf pan with parchment paper, leaving a 2-inch overhang on two opposing sides. Spray the paper and exposed sides of the pan with nonstick cooking spray.

2. In a large bowl, whisk together the flour, baking powder, cinnamon, and salt.

3. In a medium bowl, combine the eggs, bananas, brown sugar, butter, and vanilla until well blended.

4. Add the banana mixture to the flour mixture and stir until just blended. Spread the batter evenly in the prepared pan.

5. Bake for 50 to 55 minutes, until the top is golden brown and a toothpick inserted in the center comes out clean. Let the bread cool in the pan on a wire rack for 10 minutes, then hold on to the paper overhang to transfer it directly to the rack to cool completely. Remove the paper and serve.

tips

An equal amount of coconut palm sugar can be used in place of the brown sugar.

Tent the bread with foil during the last 10 minutes of baking if the bread becomes too brown.

make it vegan!

Replace the eggs with 2 psyllium "eggs" (page 18) and replace the butter with an equal amount of melted virgin coconut oil or neutral vegetable oil.

hummus

Ditch the store-bought hummus in favor of this DIY version that is uber-creamy and a cinch to prepare. One of the secrets to super-smooth hummus is the removal of the papery-thin skins around the chickpeas, a laborious, time-intensive task. The dried chickpeas used to make chickpea flour are already skinless, which means the ultimate hummus is within your grasp (with minimal effort). You can never go wrong with the classic flavorings, but if you're feeling bold, give some of the variations a spin.

MAKES 3 CUPS HUMMUS

2⅓ cups water, plus more as needed

¾ cup (90 grams) chickpea flour

¾ teaspoon fine sea salt

½ cup well-stirred tahini

⅓ cup fresh lemon juice

¼ cup extra-virgin olive oil, plus more as needed

4 cloves garlic, mashed

1 teaspoon ground cumin

¼ teaspoon cayenne pepper

1. Bring the water to a boil in a medium saucepan set over medium-high heat. Whisk in the flour and salt. Cook for 1 minute, whisking constantly. Reduce the heat to medium-low; cook, whisking, for 4 to 5 minutes longer, until thickened. Remove the pan from the heat and let the chickpea mixture cool to room temperature.

2. Transfer the cooled chickpea mixture to a food processor. Add the tahini, lemon juice, olive oil, garlic, cumin, and cayenne; process until smooth and blended. If the hummus is too stiff, add 2 to 3 additional tablespoons water until smooth and creamy.

3. Transfer the hummus to a bowl, cover, and let stand at room temperature for at least 1 hour. Adjust the seasonings (salt, cayenne, or lemon juice) to taste. Drizzle with olive oil before serving, if desired.

VARIATIONS

Roasted Pepper Hummus: Reduce the water to 1¾ cups, chickpea flour to ⅔ cup, lemon juice to 2 tablespoons, and olive oil to 3 tablespoons. Add ⅔ cup coarsely chopped roasted red peppers (from a jar, drained) along with the tahini.

B'ummus: Reduce the water to 1½ cups, chickpea flour to ½ cup, lemon juice to 2 tablespoons, and olive oil to 3 tablespoons. Add 1 cup coarsely chopped cooked beets along with the tahini.

Pumpkin Hummus: Reduce the water to 1½ cups, chickpea flour to ½ cup, lemon juice to 2 tablespoons, and olive oil to 3 tablespoons. Add ¾ cup canned pumpkin purée and ¼ teaspoon ground cinnamon along with the tahini. Garnish the hummus with ½ cup toasted pepitas (green pumpkin seeds) before serving, if desired.

California Hummus: Add ⅓ cup packed fresh basil leaves along with the tahini. Stir in ⅔ cup finely chopped, drained, oil-packed sundried tomatoes to the finished hummus.

Chipotle Lime Hummus: Omit the cumin. Replace the lemon juice with an equal amount of fresh lime juice. Add 1 whole chipotle chile (from a can, packed in adobo sauce) and 2 teaspoons finely grated lime zest along with the tahini. Garnish the hummus with chopped fresh cilantro leaves before serving, if desired.

Sriracha and Mint Hummus: Omit the cumin. Add ⅓ cup packed fresh mint leaves and 1 tablespoon sriracha sauce along with the tahini. Drizzle the hummus with additional sriracha before serving, if desired.

Za'atar Hummus: Prepare za'atar on page 94. Sprinkle hummus with 1 to 2 tablespoons za'atar, along with a drizzle of olive oil, before serving.

tip
Slice the cloves of garlic in half lengthwise before mashing; if they have green germs/ sprouts in the center, remove them. This removes any harsh bite or burn that is often associated with raw garlic.

storage tip
Store in an airtight container in the refrigerator for up to 2 weeks.

roasted chickpea butter

Introducing your new favorite alternative to nut butters. Roasting the chickpea flour in butter—or coconut oil or olive oil for a dairy-free option—gives it a deep, nutty flavor that is rounded out with the subtle sweetness of coconut palm sugar. Spread (or slather) it just as you would peanut butter, or eat it straight off of the spoon. **MAKES 1¾ CUPS**

8 tablespoons (1 stick) unsalted butter
1 cup (120 grams) chickpea flour

¾ teaspoon fine sea salt
2¾ cups boiling water
¼ cup coconut palm sugar

1 teaspoon vanilla extract

1. Melt the butter in a medium saucepan set over medium heat. Whisk in the flour and salt. Cook, whisking, for 2 minutes, until blended and smooth. Continue to cook, constantly stirring with a rubber spatula or wooden spoon, for 6 to 8 minutes longer, until the mixture is the color of dark caramel.

2. Slowly add the boiling water, whisking until completely blended and smooth. Add the coconut sugar; continue whisking for 7 to 8 minutes longer, until the mixture is very thick and is the consistency of a thick pudding (but not as thick as peanut butter). Remove the pan from the heat and cool the chickpea mixture to room temperature.

3. Transfer the cooled chickpea mixture to a food processor. Add the vanilla; process until blended and creamy. If the mixture is too stiff, add 1 to 2 additional tablespoons water until the butter is smooth and creamy.

4. Transfer the chickpea butter to an airtight container. Store in the refrigerator and use as a spread in the same manner as peanut butter.

tips
Have the boiling water ready to use when whisking the chickpea flour–butter mixture so that you can add it as soon as the mixture is the right color (the mixture darkens quickly toward the end).

An equal amount of your favorite sweetener (e.g., honey, maple syrup, natural cane sugar, packed brown sugar) can be used in place of the coconut sugar.

make it vegan!
Use an equal amount of virgin coconut oil or olive oil in place of the butter.

Sugar-Free Chickpea Butter: Omit the coconut sugar and add an extra 2 tablespoons of water. Add stevia (powdered or liquid) to taste, along with the vanilla.

Roasted Chickpea Cookie Spread: Increase the total amount of coconut sugar to ⅔ cup, increase the vanilla to 1 tablespoon and add ½ teaspoon ground cinnamon along with the vanilla. If desired, add ⅓ cup finely chopped semisweet chocolate.

Coconut Chickpea Butter: Use virgin coconut oil in place of the butter. Reduce the boiling water to 1¾ cups and add 1 cup well-stirred full-fat coconut milk. Increase the coconut sugar to 6 tablespoons.

Crunchy Chickpea Butter: Chop 1¼ cups canned chickpeas (rinsed and drained); dry thoroughly on paper towels. Place the chickpeas in a 9-inch pie plate; toss with 2 teaspoons vegetable oil and a pinch of salt. Spread evenly. Bake in a 350°F oven for 15 to 20 minutes, until golden brown and dry. Cool completely in the pan. Stir into the chickpea butter.

storage tip
Store in an airtight container in the refrigerator for up to 1 month.

garlic & sweet chile chickpea chips

Chips are party stalwarts, but you can enjoy these healthy chickpea flour chips anytime you please. **MAKES 6 SERVINGS (64 CHIPS)**

2 cups (240 grams) chickpea flour

1 teaspoon fine sea salt

2 tablespoons extra-virgin olive oil

3 cloves garlic, mashed

1 tablespoon sriracha sauce

1 tablespoon coconut palm sugar

½ cup warm (not hot) water

1. Preheat the oven to 350°F. Position the oven racks in the middle and upper-middle positions.

2. In a food processor, process the flour and salt until blended. Add the oil, garlic, sriracha, and coconut sugar; process for 30 seconds. Add the water and process until the mixture comes together into a ball.

3. Roll the dough into a uniform log; cut the log into 8 equal pieces. Roll each piece into a ball. Place one dough ball on a medium-size piece (about half the size of the baking sheet) of parchment paper. Place a second medium-size piece of parchment paper on top of the dough. Using a rolling pin, roll the dough into a ⅛-inch-thick circle (it will be about 7- to 8-inches in diameter); remove the top parchment sheet and cut the dough into 8 equal wedges. Transfer the parchment with the wedges to one end of a large baking sheet. Repeat with 3 more of the dough balls, covering 2 baking sheets.

4. Bake for 8 minutes; switch the baking sheets' positions from the upper and lower racks. Bake for 5 to 9 minutes longer, until the chips are golden brown and appear crispy. Transfer the chips directly onto a wire rack with a spatula to cool completely. Repeat with the remaining dough.

tip
An equal amount of packed brown sugar or natural cane sugar can be used in place of the coconut sugar.

Garlic Bread Chickpea Chips: Omit the sriracha and sugar. Add an extra tablespoon of warm water. Add 2 tablespoons grated Parmesan cheese (or nutritional yeast flakes to make it vegan) along with the salt.

Cracked Pepper Chickpea Chips: Omit the garlic, sriracha, and coconut sugar. Add an extra tablespoon of warm water. Add 2½ teaspoons freshly cracked black pepper along with the salt.

BBQ Chickpea Chips: Omit the garlic, sriracha, and coconut sugar and reduce the water to ⅓ cup. Add 3½ tablespoons prepared barbecue sauce along with the water.

Cheddar Beer Chickpea Chips: Omit the coconut sugar and sriracha; reduce the garlic to 1 clove. Replace the water with an equal amount of room temperature beer (gluten-free) and add 1 cup finely shredded sharp Cheddar cheese (or nondairy Cheddar cheese to make it vegan) along with the oil.

storage tip

Store the chips in an airtight tin at room temperature for up to 3 days.

chocolate truffle spread

This indulgent spread takes it cue from chocolate hazelnut spread, but without the nuts, dairy, and copious amounts of sugar. **MAKES ABOUT 2 CUPS**

1½ cups well-stirred full-fat coconut milk
1 cup water
⅔ cup coconut palm sugar

7 tablespoons unsweetened natural cocoa powder
6 tablespoons (45 grams) chickpea flour
¼ teaspoon fine sea salt

⅓ cup virgin coconut oil
2 teaspoons vanilla extract
2 teaspoons instant espresso powder (optional)

1. In a medium saucepan, combine the coconut milk, water, coconut sugar, cocoa powder, flour, and salt. Cook over medium heat for 7 to 9 minutes, whisking until blended, smooth, and thickened.

2. Remove the pan from the heat and whisk in the coconut oil (it does not need to be completely blended); let the mixture cool to room temperature.

3. Transfer the cooled chickpea mixture to a food processor. Add the vanilla and espresso powder; process until blended and creamy.

4. Transfer the spread to an airtight container. Store in the refrigerator and use as a spread in the same manner as chocolate-hazelnut spread.

tips
An equal amount of unsalted butter can be used in place of the coconut oil.

An equal amount of packed brown sugar or natural cane sugar can be used in place of the coconut sugar.

An equal amount of dairy or other nondairy milk can be used in place of the coconut milk.

storage tip
Store in an airtight container in the refrigerator for up to 1 month.

sweet potato chickpea tortilla chips

Sweet potatoes give these chips a gorgeous glow, while chickpea flour and flaxseed meal contribute great crunch. The sum total is a snack replete with both tremendous flavor and nutrients. **MAKES 4 TO 6 SERVINGS (ABOUT 64 CHIPS)**

4 cups peeled, coarsely chopped sweet potatoes

1 cup coarsely chopped onion

1 cup (120 grams) chickpea flour

1 cup flaxseed meal (ground flaxseeds)

2½ tablespoons olive oil

1 tablespoon fresh lime juice

1 tablespoon chili powder

1¼ teaspoons fine sea salt

1. Preheat the oven to 225°F.

2. In a food processor, process the sweet potatoes and onion until very finely chopped (almost smooth). Add the flour, flaxseed meal, olive oil, lime juice, chili powder, and salt. Pulse until the mixture comes together into a cohesive dough. Let it rest at room temperature for 10 minutes.

3. Place one half of the dough on a large piece of parchment paper. Place a second large piece of parchment paper on top of the dough. Using a rolling pin, roll the dough to a ¼-inch thickness. Using a sharp knife or pizza cutter, score the dough into squares; score the squares in half on the diagonal to make triangles.

4. Place the parchment paper with the scored dough on a large baking sheet. Repeat with the remaining dough, placing it on a second baking sheet.

5. Bake for 1 hour. Slide the chips off of the parchment paper, placing them directly on the baking sheets (discard the parchment paper). Break chips along the score lines and turn over. Bake for 50 to 65 minutes longer, until completely dry and crisp. Transfer the chips to wire racks to cool completely.

storage tip
Store the chips in an airtight container for up to 2 weeks.

VARIATION

Flaming Tortilla Chips: Add ¼ teaspoon to 1 teaspoon (or more!) cayenne pepper along with the chili powder.

za'atar chickpea crackers

If you've given up grains, crackers may seem out of the question. But no longer, thanks to chickpea flour. A short list of ingredients comprise the basic cracker, and then you are free to add just about any flavors or toppings that suit your fancy. For example, za'atar, an Arabic blend of thyme, marjoram, sesame seeds, and sumac, elevates these crispy bites from great to grand. **MAKES ABOUT 48 CRACKERS**

ZA'ATAR
2 tablespoons dried thyme leaves
2 tablespoons toasted sesame seeds
1 tablespoon dried marjoram leaves

1 tablespoon sumac or finely grated lemon zest
½ teaspoon fine sea salt

CRACKERS
2 cups (240 grams) chickpea flour

1 teaspoon baking powder
1 teaspoon fine sea salt
¼ cup olive oil
7 to 8 tablespoons warm (not hot) water

1. To make the za'atar, coarsely grind the thyme, sesame seeds, marjoram, sumac, and salt with a mortar and pestle.

2. To make the crackers, preheat the oven to 350°F. Line a large baking sheet with parchment paper.

3. In a food processor, process the flour, baking powder, and salt until blended. Add the oil; pulse until the mixture resembles moist sand. With the motor running, drizzle in 4 tablespoons of the water; add an additional 3 to 4 tablespoons of water until the mixture just comes together into a ball. Divide the dough in half.

4. Place half the dough on a large piece of parchment paper. Place a second large piece of parchment paper on top of dough. Using a rolling pin, roll the dough to a ⅛-inch thickness. Using a 2-inch round cookie cutter or biscuit cutter, cut out the crackers and place them on the prepared baking sheet. Re-roll dough scraps and cut out the rest.

5. Sprinkle each cracker with a small amount of za'atar, gently pressing it into the dough.

6. Bake for 14 to 18 minutes, until golden brown. Transfer the crackers directly onto a wire rack with a spatula to cool completely. Repeat with the remaining dough and za'atar.

tips

You can cut the dough into larger or smaller shapes. Increase the baking time by several minutes for larger crackers and reduce the baking time for smaller crackers. Additionally, be sure to bake like-size pieces together to ensure even baking.

Unlike doughs made from wheat flour, this dough can be rolled and re-rolled as many times as you please while still yielding crisp-tender crackers.

vegetables & sides

panisses (chickpea french fries)

These addictive morsels—which some contend are the "original" French fries—hail from the South of France (specifically Marseille). Both crisp and creamy, they are out-of-this-world good. I've given options to either fry or broil them, after which you can give them the traditional treatment: a light shower of sea salt and pepper plus a squeeze of fresh lemon juice. Alternatively, serve them with your favorite dipping sauce (like the Pepita Romesco on page 129). **MAKES 4 SERVINGS**

Olive oil for greasing pan, frying, or broiling

1 cup (120 grams) chickpea flour

1 teaspoon fine sea salt

2 cups water

2 teaspoons olive oil

Freshly ground black pepper

Lemon wedges, for serving

1. Grease the bottom and sides of a 9-inch square baking pan with olive oil.

2. In a medium bowl, whisk the flour and salt together. Whisk in 1 cup of the water and the olive oil until blended and smooth.

3. In a medium saucepan, bring the remaining 1 cup water to a boil. Reduce the heat to medium and whisk in the batter. Cook, stirring constantly, for 2 to 4 minutes, until the batter is very thick. Immediately pour and spread it into the prepared pan; use a spatula dipped in warm water to smooth the top.

4. Cool the mixture to room temperature then place in the refrigerator, loosely covered, for at least 1 hour or for up to 24 hours. Invert it onto a cutting board and cut it into ¼-inch-wide batons.

5. There are two ways to cook the panisses. To fry them, heat ¼ inch of olive oil in a large skillet. When the oil is hot (add a small test piece to skillet; it should bubble immediately), add about a third of the fries, taking care not to overcrowd the pan. Cook for 1 to 2 minutes, until the bottoms are golden brown; turn them over with tongs or a spatula and cook for 1 to 2 minutes longer, until deep golden brown. Transfer the fries to a paper towel-lined plate to drain; repeat with the remaining fries, heating more oil in the pan as needed.

6. Alternatively, to broil the panisses, position the broiler rack in the oven 8 inches from the heat source. Grease a large rimmed baking sheet with olive oil and place it on the rack to preheat, 3 minutes. Using an oven mitt (sheet will be very hot), remove the sheet from the oven. Arrange the panisses on the sheet. Broil for 3 to 5 minutes, until golden brown. Remove from the oven and flip the panisses over with a spatula. Broil for 3 to 5 minutes longer, until the other sides are golden brown.

7. Season the panisses with salt and pepper and squeeze the lemon wedges over them. Serve hot.

VARIATIONS

Italian Panelle: Prepare the panisses as directed, but add 2 cloves garlic, minced, to the batter along with the olive oil. Spread the batter into an 8-inch square pan (so that mixture is thicker when firm). Cut the chilled panelle into 16 rectangular pieces and cook as directed (fry or broil).

Panelle Sandwiches: Prepare panelle as directed above but cut the block of chilled batter into 4 equal squares and cook as directed (fry or broil). Serve on gluten-free buns or bread as you would a burger with the topping of your choice.

power-veggie fritters

What the world needs now is vegetables, more delicious vegetables. It's not the only thing that the world has too little of, but most of us could sure use a boost. These fritters deliver. You can make them with any combination of vegetables, herbs, and seasonings you love, plus, the cooked, cooled fritters can be stored in the refrigerator for a quick hit of vegetables anytime (they are delicious warm, cold, or at room temperature). The chickpea flour in the batter leads to perfectly cooked, extra-crispy, flavorful fritters every time. **MAKES 20 FRITTERS**

2 large eggs
¼ cup warm (not hot) water
¾ cup (90 grams) chickpea flour
3 cloves garlic, minced
¾ teaspoon fine sea salt

¾ teaspoon baking soda
¼ teaspoon freshly ground black pepper
3 cups finely shredded vegetables (such as sweet potatoes, zucchini, carrots, parsnips, or beets)

1 cup finely chopped broccoli or cauliflower
½ cup freshly grated Parmesan cheese
5 teaspoons olive oil

1. Preheat the oven to 250°F.

2. In a large bowl, whisk the eggs, water, flour, garlic, salt, baking soda, and pepper until blended and smooth. Stir in the shredded vegetables, broccoli, and Parmesan cheese.

3. Heat 1 teaspoon of the olive oil in a large nonstick skillet over medium-low heat. Scoop four ¼-cup-size mounds of batter into the skillet, pressing down slightly to flatten. Cook 2½ to 3 minutes on each side, flipping once with a spatula and pressing down again to flatten, until golden brown and cooked through.

4. Transfer the finished fritters to a paper towel-lined plate to drain and then place on an ungreased baking sheet in the oven to stay warm, keeping them in a single layer to maintain crispness. Repeat with the remaining oil and batter. Serve warm.

make it vegan!
Replace the Parmesan cheese with ⅓ cup nutritional yeast flakes and replace the eggs with 2 psyllium "eggs" (page 18).

storage tip
Store the cooled fritters in an airtight container in the refrigerator for up to 5 days. Reheat in the microwave on a paper towel for 12 to 15 seconds. Alternatively, enjoy cold or at room temperature.

karane (savory chickpea flan)

Karane is a popular street food found in the markets of eastern Morocco as well as in neighboring Algeria. When purchased from carts, it is typically served warm on crusty, French-style baguettes, then sprinkled with cumin and chili powder. I've added the spices directly to the flan, and suggest serving it in place of mashed potatoes.

MAKES 6 SERVINGS

3 tablespoons olive oil, plus more for pan

1 cup (120 grams) chickpea flour

1½ cups water

2 large eggs

2 cloves garlic, mashed to a paste

1¼ teaspoons fine sea salt

1 teaspoon hot smoked paprika

1 teaspoon ground cumin

6 cups tender watercress sprigs

2 teaspoons fresh lemon juice

1. Preheat the oven to 350°F. Grease an 8-inch square baking pan with olive oil.

2. In a large bowl, whisk the flour and water until blended and smooth. Whisk in the eggs, 2 tablespoons of the olive oil, the garlic, 1 teaspoon of the salt, and the paprika; pour into the prepared pan.

3. Bake for 30 to 35 minutes, until the flan is just set but still jiggles slightly at the center when the pan is gently shaken. Transfer to a wire rack and cool for 15 minutes or completely.

4. In a large bowl, toss the watercress with the lemon juice and the remaining tablespoon of olive oil and ¼ teaspoon salt. Cut the karane into 6 servings. Divide the watercress among the plates and top with portions of the karane.

baked coconut chickpea onion rings

I'm admittedly infatuated with onion rings, and while I'll never tire of the crunchy deliciousness of deep-fried versions, I think my baked, coconut-chickpea version is even better. Chickpea flour gives oven-baked vegetables a crispy-crunchy finish, so you won't miss the deep-frying one bit. And even though people don't often associate coconut with onion rings, this recipe will convince them that they are an ideal match.

MAKES 4 SERVINGS

Nonstick cooking spray
1½ cups (180 grams) chickpea flour
1 teaspoon fine sea salt
⅛ teaspoon freshly ground black pepper
1 large egg
½ cup dairy or nondairy milk
1 cup unsweetened flaked coconut, finely chopped
2 large sweet onions

1. Preheat the oven to 450°F. Grease 2 large baking sheets with nonstick cooking spray.

2. In a shallow dish, combine ¾ cup of the flour, ½ teaspoon of the salt, and the pepper. In a second shallow dish, whisk together the egg and milk until well blended. In a third shallow dish, mix together the coconut and the remaining ¾ cup flour and ½ teaspoon salt.

3. Peel the onions, trimming off the ends; cut them crosswise into ¼-inch-thick slices. Break the onion slices into individual rings.

4. Dredge each ring in the flour mixture, then dip in the egg mixture and gently shake off the excess. Press the ring into the coconut mixture, coating all sides; transfer to the prepared sheet. Repeat with the remaining rings. Spray the rings with cooking spray.

5. Bake for 10 minutes; using a spatula, flip the rings. Switch the baking sheets' positions from the upper and lower racks and bake for 8 to 12 minutes longer, until golden brown and crispy. Serve immediately.

tip
Create extra room on the baking sheet by placing small onion rings in the space inside larger onion rings (make sure the rings do not touch).

VARIATION

Salt and Pepper Onion Rings: Omit the coconut. Increase the black pepper to ½ teaspoon.

zucchini-chickpea tots

My mother was (and still is) a very health-conscious cook, but she would occasionally let my siblings and me pick out TV dinners when they went out for dinner. My selection had a sole requirement: it had to include Tater Tots. Although Tater Tots and TV dinners are no longer on my menu, my zucchini-chickpea tots are. Golden-brown, crispy, and a little bit cheesy (both literally and figuratively), they will make you crave zucchini like never before. **MAKES 6 SERVINGS**

2 cups packed shredded zucchini

2 large eggs

½ cup (60 grams) chickpea flour

½ teaspoon fine sea salt

¼ teaspoon baking soda

⅛ teaspoon freshly ground black pepper

½ cup finely chopped onion

½ cup grated Parmesan cheese

1. Preheat the oven to 400°F. Line a large baking sheet with parchment paper.

2. Place the zucchini in a clean kitchen towel. Twist the ends together and squeeze as much excess liquid from the zucchini as possible; discard liquid.

3. In a large bowl, whisk together the eggs, flour, salt, baking soda, and pepper until blended and smooth. Stir in the onion, Parmesan cheese, and zucchini until blended.

4. Drop heaping tablespoons of the batter onto the prepared baking sheet (mixture will be somewhat wet). With moistened fingertips, press each mound into an oval shape.

5. Bake for 10 to 12 minutes, until golden brown. Serve warm.

tip
Other varieties of squash, such as yellow (crookneck) squash or pattypan squash can be used in place of the zucchini.

make it vegan!
Replace the eggs with 2 psyllium "eggs" (page 18) and replace the Parmesan with ⅓ cup nutritional yeast flakes.

roasted vegetables with lemon chickpea aioli

I've never been a fan of jarred mayonnaise, but homemade versions—whether you call them aioli or mayonnaise—are something else entirely. Luscious, rich, and deeply flavorful (thanks to a perfect balance of extra-virgin olive oil, garlic, and lemon), it makes everything from vegetables to sandwiches to appetizers irresistible. My only problem? The raw egg yolks that deliver aioli's signature unctuousness. So now I am thrilled to present my solution: an egg-free, dairy-free aioli made with—you guessed it—chickpea flour. Make it ASAP, as I am certain you will be as thrilled as I am. Better still, prepare the roasted vegetables to showcase the rich flavor and silken texture of the aioli. **MAKES 8 SERVINGS (ABOUT 1 CUP AIOLI)**

LEMON CHICKPEA AIOLI
½ cup water
3 tablespoons (22.5 grams) chickpea flour
¼ teaspoon fine sea salt
⅓ cup extra-virgin olive oil
1 teaspoon finely grated lemon zest
1 tablespoon fresh lemon juice

1¼ teaspoons Dijon mustard
1 small clove garlic, mashed into a paste
Pinch of cayenne pepper

ROASTED VEGETABLES
1½ pounds small red or gold potatoes, scrubbed and quartered

2 bunches baby carrots, ends trimmed
3 tablespoons olive oil
1 teaspoon fine sea salt
2 medium red bell peppers, cut into ½-inch strips
1 pound asparagus, tough ends trimmed
1 bunch green onions, ends trimmed

1. To make the aioli, bring the water to a boil in a small saucepan set over medium-high heat. Whisk in the flour and salt. Cook for 1 minute, whisking constantly. Reduce the heat to medium-low; cook, whisking, for 4 to 5 minutes longer, until thickened. Transfer the mixture to a small, heatproof bowl; cover and refrigerate until cold.

2. Transfer the cold chickpea mixture to a food processor or blender. Add the olive oil, lemon zest, lemon juice, mustard, garlic, and cayenne; process until blended and very creamy. Transfer to a small covered container and refrigerate until ready to use.

tips
Slice the clove of garlic in half lengthwise before using; if there is a green germ/sprout in the center, remove it. This removes any harsh bite or burn that is often associated with raw garlic.

If baby carrots are not available, use 5 or 6 regular carrots, cut into approximately 2½ by ½-inch sticks.

egyptian carrot & fresh herb salad

The secret to this fresh and flavorful salad is twofold: first is the addition of *dukkah* to the dressing, which adds spice, depth of flavor, and a bit of creaminess (thanks to the chickpea flour). The second is using the freshest carrots—sweet and free of any bitterness—that you can find. **MAKES 6 SERVINGS**

3 tablespoons extra-virgin olive oil

3 tablespoons Sunflower-Chickpea Dukkah (page 119)

2 tablespoons fresh lemon juice

2 cloves garlic, mashed

¼ teaspoon ground cinnamon

Fine sea salt

Cayenne pepper

5 cups shredded carrots

¼ cup packed fresh cilantro leaves, chopped

¼ cup packed fresh mint leaves, chopped

⅓ cup dried currants or raisins

1. In a small bowl, whisk together the olive oil, 1 tablespoon of the dukkah, the lemon juice, garlic, and cinnamon. Season to taste with salt and cayenne.

2. In a large bowl, combine the carrots, cilantro, mint, and currants. Add the dressing and toss gently to coat.

3. Cover the salad and refrigerate for at least 1 hour, until chilled, or for up to 4 hours. Sprinkle with the remaining 2 tablespoons dukkah just before serving.

tip
This dressing can be used for all varieties of fresh vegetable salads.

butternut squash & chard salad with sunflower-chickpea dukkah

Sweet roasted squash, fresh and earthy Swiss chard, and a toasted chickpea *dukkah* are an irresistible trio in this gorgeous autumnal salad. **MAKES 6 SERVINGS**

1 large butternut squash, peeled and cut into 1-inch dice
4½ tablespoons extra-virgin olive oil
Fine sea salt and freshly ground black pepper

2 teaspoons fresh lemon juice
1 teaspoon honey
1 large bunch red Swiss chard, ribs removed, leaves thinly sliced crosswise (about 6 cups)

3 tablespoons Sunflower-Chickpea Dukkah (recipe follows)

1. Preheat the oven to 450°F.

2. On a large rimmed baking sheet, toss the butternut squash with 1½ table-spoons of the oil. Season it with salt and pepper and spread it in a single layer. Roast the squash for 25 to 30 minutes, stirring occasionally, until the squash is tender. Let it cool in the pan for 10 minutes.

3. In a small bowl, whisk together the remaining 3 tablespoons oil, the lemon juice, and the honey; season with salt and pepper to taste.

4. In a large bowl, combine the Swiss chard and the squash. Add the dressing and the dukkah; toss gently to coat.

tip
An equal amount of very thinly sliced, trimmed kale leaves can be used in place of the Swiss chard.

make it vegan!
Replace the honey with an equal amount of maple syrup, natural cane sugar, or coconut palm sugar.

Sunflower-Chickpea Dukkah

Dukkah is an Egyptian spice blend comprised of toasted spices and finely chopped nuts and seeds. Here I've left out the nuts in favor of sunflower and sesame seeds and added toasted chickpea flour, another common addition to the boldly flavored blend. Mix it with olive oil and serve as an accompaniment to grain-free breads or as a dip for vegetables, or use the *dukkah* as is to season everything from vegetables to sauces to salads. MAKES ABOUT 1 CUP

⅔ cup sunflower seeds
⅓ cup sesame seeds
½ cup (60 grams) chickpea flour
1 tablespoon ground coriander
1 tablespoon ground cumin
1 teaspoon fine sea salt
2 teaspoons freshly ground black pepper

1. Preheat the oven to 350°F. Spread the sunflower seeds and sesame seeds on a large rimmed baking sheet. Bake for 3 to 6 minutes, until toasted. Transfer the seeds to a food processor.

2. In a large skillet, cook the chickpea flour, stirring, over medium-high heat for 4 to 5 minutes, until fragrant and deep golden brown. Add the flour to the seeds in the food processor. Wipe out the skillet.

3. Add the coriander and cumin to the skillet; cook and stir over medium heat for 30 to 60 seconds, until aromatic. Transfer to the food processor. Allow all contents of the food processor to cool completely.

4. Add the salt and pepper and pulse the mixture to a fine or coarse texture (according to preference); be careful not to over-process or it will turn into a paste. Store in an airtight jar or container for up to 6 months.

baked eggplant fries

French fry fans, take note: fries made with eggplant, a coating of chickpea flour, and a hot blast in the oven are every bit as delectable, if not more so. The eggplant keeps its shape in "fry" form, but then melts in your mouth. **MAKES 4 SERVINGS**

1 medium (12-ounce) globe eggplant
1 tablespoon olive oil
½ cup (60 grams) chickpea flour

⅓ cup freshly grated Parmesan cheese
¾ teaspoon fine sea salt
½ teaspoon freshly ground black pepper

1 large egg, at room temperature
Olive oil cooking spray
1 cup good-quality prepared marinara sauce

1. Preheat the oven to 450°F. Line 2 large baking sheets with parchment paper.

2. Trim the ends of the eggplant. Cut lengthwise into ¼-inch-thick slices, then into 1¼-inch-thick sticks. Place them in a large bowl and toss with olive oil to coat.

3. In a shallow dish or plate, combine the flour, Parmesan cheese, salt, and pepper. In another shallow dish or plate, whisk the egg with a fork until well blended.

4. Working with 3 to 4 fries at a time, dip the eggplant in the egg, shaking off the excess; dredge in the flour mixture, turning to coat. Using a fork, transfer the eggplant to the prepared baking sheets. Spray the eggplant with the cooking spray.

5. Bake for 9 minutes. Using a spatula or fork, carefully turn over the eggplant. Bake for 4 to 6 minutes longer, until golden brown. Serve hot with the marinara sauce for dipping.

VARIATION

Zucchini Fries: Use 12 ounces zucchini (3 to 4 medium zucchini) in place of the eggplant.

tips

Cut the eggplant fries to the same size so that they cook evenly.

It is much easier to whisk the egg when it is at room temperature than when it is cold from the refrigerator. You can warm it quickly by placing it in a bowl of warm (not hot) water for 1 to 2 minutes.

make it vegan!

Replace the egg with 1 psyllium "egg" (page 18) whisked with an additional tablespoon of water, and replace the Parmesan with an equal amount of nutritional yeast flakes.

tandoori roasted cauliflower

If it's a wow-worthy vegetable dish you're after, this is it. Roasting the cauliflower brings out its natural sweetness, a delicious foil to the spicy, crispy-crunch of the topping. **MAKES 4 SERVINGS**

⅓ cup plain yogurt

¼ cup (30 grams) chickpea flour

3 cloves garlic

2 tablespoons peeled, coarsely chopped fresh ginger

2 tablespoons olive oil, plus more for pan

1½ tablespoons paprika

2 teaspoons ground cumin

1 teaspoon fine sea salt

¼ teaspoon cayenne pepper

¼ teaspoon freshly ground black pepper

6 cups small cauliflower florets (about 1 large head)

½ cup packed fresh mint leaves, chopped, for serving

Lime wedges, for serving

1. In a food processor or blender, process the yogurt, flour, garlic, ginger, 2 tablespoons olive oil, paprika, cumin, salt, cayenne pepper, and black pepper until smooth.

2. Grease a large, rimmed baking sheet with olive oil. In a large bowl, toss the cauliflower with the yogurt mixture. Use your hands to rub and push the marinade into the crevices of the florets. Spread the cauliflower in a single layer on the prepared baking sheet. Let it stand at room temperature for 30 minutes.

3. Preheat the oven to 425°F. Roast the cauliflower for 35 to 40 minutes, stirring once or twice, until tender. Let it cool slightly in the pan on a wire rack. Sprinkle with mint and serve with lime wedges.

make it vegan!
Use an equal amount of plain nondairy yogurt (e.g., coconut yogurt) in place of the yogurt. Alternatively, use ¼ cup well-stirred full-fat coconut milk mixed with 1½ tablespoons fresh lemon or lime juice.

cherry tomato & thyme gratin

Besides popping them in my mouth whole, this is one of my favorite ways to savor cherry tomatoes. The chickpea flour crumble becomes golden and crispy in no time, while the tomatoes beneath literally burst with fresh flavor. **MAKES 4 SERVINGS**

⅔ cup (80 grams) chickpea flour

2 cloves garlic, minced

1 teaspoon natural cane sugar

¾ teaspoon fine sea salt

¼ teaspoon freshly ground black pepper

5 tablespoons extra-virgin olive oil

⅓ cup freshly grated Parmesan cheese

4 cups cherry tomatoes

½ teaspoon dried thyme

¼ cup packed fresh, flat-leaf parsley leaves, chopped

1. In a medium bowl, whisk the flour, garlic, sugar, ¼ teaspoon salt, and ⅛ teaspoon pepper. Add 4 tablespoons of the olive oil. Mix with a fork until it resembles moist sand. Stir in the Parmesan cheese. Refrigerate for 15 minutes.

2. Preheat the oven to 400°F. Place the cherry tomatoes in a 9-inch square baking pan. Add the thyme, the remaining tablespoon of oil, ½ teaspoon salt, and ⅛ teaspoon pepper; toss to combine. Bake for 20 minutes.

3. Stir the parsley into the chickpea flour mixture; sprinkle the mixture over the tomatoes. Bake for 20 to 25 minutes longer, until the topping is golden brown. Serve hot or warm.

make it vegan!
Replace the Parmesan cheese with ¼ cup nutritional yeast flakes.

entrees

skillet pizza with figs, goat cheese & arugula

Prepare to meet your new favorite pizza. The crust is ridiculously simple, yet crispy-crunchy fantastic, and the combination of toppings—sweet figs, bittersweet arugula, and tangy goat cheese—will make you weak in the knees. But this crust, like any pizza crust, can be topped with any combination of ingredients you can dream up. You may never order takeout again. **MAKES 4 SERVINGS**

CRUST
1 cup (120 grams) chickpea flour
¼ teaspoon fine sea salt
1 cup warm (not hot) water
3 tablespoons olive oil
2 cloves garlic, minced

TOPPINGS
½ cup moist dried figs, ends trimmed, sliced crosswise
4 ounces soft goat cheese, crumbled
2½ cups fresh baby arugula leaves

1 tablespoon extra-virgin olive oil
1 teaspoon fresh lemon juice
Fine sea salt and freshly ground black pepper
2 teaspoons finely grated lemon zest

1. To make the crust, whisk the flour and salt together in a medium bowl. Add the warm water, 2 tablespoons olive oil, and the garlic, whisking until blended and smooth. Let the batter stand at room temperature for at least 1 hour.

2. When you're ready to cook the pizza, position the broiler rack in the oven 8 inches from the heat source. Place a 10-inch cast iron skillet on the rack to preheat for 10 minutes.

3. Using an oven mitt (the skillet will be very, very hot), remove the skillet from the oven. Add the remaining tablespoon olive oil to the skillet; swirl to coat the bottom. Pour in the batter; broil for 4 to 7 minutes, until the center of the crust is just set and the edges are golden brown.

storage tip
Store the tofu in an airtight
container in the refrigerator
for up to 2 weeks.

Burmese Tofu Salad: Press about 1¼ cups Burmese tofu, cut into 1-inch cubes (about ¼ of the recipe), between a double layer of paper towels to remove excess moisture. Chop into very small pieces. In a small bowl, mix 2 tablespoons mayonnaise (regular or vegan), 2 teaspoons sweet pickle relish, and ½ teaspoon Dijon mustard until blended. Add the tofu and ¼ cup finely chopped celery. Makes 1 to 2 servings.

Burmese Tofu, Bok Choy, and Mushroom Soup: In a medium saucepan, combine 2 cloves minced garlic, 1 tablespoon minced fresh ginger, 4 cups chicken or vegetable broth, 1 tablespoon cider vinegar, and 2 teaspoons toasted sesame oil. Bring to a boil over medium-high heat. Stir in 8 ounces sliced mushrooms; reduce heat and simmer for 5 minutes. Stir in 1¼ cups Burmese tofu cut into 1-inch cubes (about ¼ of the recipe), 3 cups sliced bok choy, and ¼ cup chopped green onions; simmer for 3 to 4 minutes or until bok choy is wilted and tofu is heated through. Makes 2 servings.

Stir-Fried Burmese Tofu: In a small bowl, whisk together 2 tablespoons chicken or vegetable broth, 1 teaspoon dark molasses, 1 clove minced garlic, 1 teaspoon toasted sesame oil, ½ teaspoon ground ginger, and ½ teaspoon cider vinegar. Cut 2½ cups Burmese tofu into 1-inch cubes (about ½ of the recipe). Press between a double layer of paper towels to remove excess moisture. In a large skillet, heat 1 tablespoon of neutral vegetable oil over medium-high heat. Add tofu and cook, stirring, for 3 to 4 minutes or until golden brown. Transfer to a plate. Add 1 medium red bell pepper, thinly sliced, to the skillet; cook, stirring, for 2 minutes. Add the tofu, 4 cups packed baby spinach, and broth mixture to the skillet; cook, stirring, for 2 minutes until heated through and the spinach is wilted. Makes 2 servings.

Burmese Tofu and Cabbage Salad: Cut 2½ cups Burmese tofu into 1-inch cubes (about ½ of the recipe). Press between a double layer of paper towels to remove excess moisture. In a small bowl, whisk together 1 tablespoon grated fresh ginger, ½ teaspoon fine sea salt, 2 tablespoons cider vinegar, 2 tablespoons melted virgin coconut oil, and 1 tablespoon coconut palm sugar. In a large bowl, combine 3 cups thinly shredded purple cabbage, ½ cup shredded carrots, ¼ cup sliced green onions, and ¼ cup fresh basil or mint, chopped. Add tofu and dressing; gently toss to coat. Cover and refrigerate for at least 30 minutes, until chilled, or for up to 2 hours. Makes 4 servings.

baked sweet potato falafel

Like many other children, the first recipes I ever made were sweets—in my case, mostly cookies—but the first savory dish I remember making was falafel. It is a stretch to say that it was a "recipe"—it was really a falafel mix from the food co-op—but it was an exciting new adventure, and I was soon making it almost every Saturday for lunch. Making the crunchy, spicy patties is almost as easy with this recipe. Traditional falafel should be prepared with dried, soaked chickpeas, not cooked chickpeas; chickpea flour is the ideal shortcut for getting authentic flavor and texture without the fuss. Nevertheless, if you love to play with tradition, then this sweet potato version is expressly for you. **MAKES 4 SERVINGS (16 FALAFEL PATTIES)**

2 tablespoons olive oil, plus more for pan

1 cup (120 grams) chickpea flour

2 teaspoons ground cumin

½ teaspoon ground coriander (optional)

1 teaspoon fine sea salt

½ teaspoon baking soda

1 ¼ cups mashed cooked sweet potato

¼ cup hot (not boiling) water

⅓ cup finely chopped onion

½ cup packed fresh, flat-leaf parsley leaves, finely chopped

½ cup packed fresh cilantro leaves, finely chopped

3 cloves garlic, minced

1. Preheat the oven to 400°F. Grease a large baking sheet with olive oil.

2. In a large bowl, whisk the flour, cumin, coriander, salt, and baking soda together until blended. Add the sweet potato, hot water, onion, parsley, cilantro, garlic, and 1 tablespoon of the olive oil, stirring until well blended. Let the mixture stand at room temperature for 15 minutes.

3. While the mixture is cooling, place the baking sheet in the oven for 15 minutes.

4. Shape the falafel dough into 16 balls. Remove the baking sheet from the oven and arrange the falafel on it; flatten them slightly with a spatula and brush with the remaining tablespoon of olive oil.

5. Bake for 15 minutes; flip the patties over with a spatula. Bake for 12 to 15 minutes longer, until they're golden brown and crispy. Serve immediately.

tip
Sweet potatoes vary in their level of moisture. If the falafel mixture appears too dry, add a bit more water; if it appears too wet, add a bit more chickpea flour.

Baked Israeli Falafel: Omit the sweet potatoes and increase the total amount of chickpea flour to 2 cups (240 grams) and the total amount of hot water to ½ cup.

Ta'miyya (Egyptian Falafel): Omit the sweet potatoes and increase the total amount of chickpea flour to 2 cups (240 grams) and the total amount of hot water to ½ cup. Reduce the cumin to 1 teaspoon and omit the coriander. Replace the onion with ¾ cup finely chopped green onions. Increase the parsley to ¾ cup and reduce the cilantro to 1 tablespoon. Sprinkle the tops of the patties with sesame seeds (about 1 tablespoon total) before baking.

Falafel Chips: Preheat the oven to 350°F and line a large baking sheet with parchment paper. Prepare the Baked Israeli Falafel (variation) batter. Place half of the falafel dough on the prepared sheet. Using moistened hands, press and spread the dough as thinly as possible into a large rectangle; smooth with an offset spatula dipped in warm water. Using a sharp knife, score the dough into chip-size squares, rectangles, or triangles. Bake for 10 to 14 minutes (it will depend on thickness of chips), until golden brown and completely dry to the touch. Transfer to a wire rack and cool completely on baking sheet. Store the cooled chips in an airtight container for up to 2 weeks.

Piccadillo Empanadas: Omit the mango and ginger. Add ¼ cup raisins, chopped, 3 tablespoons chopped green olives, 1 teaspoon ground cumin, and ¼ teaspoon ground cinnamon to the mashed black beans.

Black Bean and Sweet Potato Empanadas: Replace the ginger with 1½ teaspoons ground cumin and replace the mango with ⅔ cup mashed cooked sweet potato.

make it vegan!
Use melted virgin coconut oil or olive oil in place of the butter.

chickpea flour pasta

Store-bought noodles can't compare to homemade, but people looking for grain-free alternatives have long been out of luck on both fronts. Chickpea flour saves the day. It's not a newfangled notion: chickpea flour has long been used to make pasta in Italy, as well as gnocchi, and spaetzle-like dumplings in North African cuisines. One innovation I've added is a bit of psyllium husk; it helps the pasta hold together while it's being shaped and cooked. **MAKES 4 TO 6 SERVINGS**

2 cups (240 grams) chickpea flour, plus more for dusting

1 tablespoon whole psyllium husks
½ teaspoon fine sea salt, plus more for pasta water

3 large eggs
1 to 3 teaspoons ice water

1. Place the flour, psyllium husks, and ½ teaspoon salt in a food processor; process until combined. Add the eggs; process for 1 minute, until the dough appears very moist and begins to clump at the sides of the bowl. If the mixture appears dry, add water, 1 teaspoon at a time, pulsing to combine. If the dough appears wet and sticky, add a few teaspoons more flour.

2. Gather the dough into a ball and knead it for 1 minute on a clean work surface lightly dusted with chickpea flour. Place the dough in a medium bowl and sprinkle it with more flour. Cover the bowl with plastic wrap and let the dough rest at room temperature for at least 30 minutes.

3. Place the dough on a clean work surface lightly dusted with chickpea flour. Cut the dough in half; cover 1 piece of dough with a clean kitchen towel.

4. Using a rolling pin dusted with flour, begin rolling the other piece of dough from the center outward, flipping it over several times to keep it from sticking. Roll it to ⅛-inch thickness.

recipe continues

make it vegan!
Omit the tablespoon of psyllium. Use three psyllium "eggs" (page 18) in place of the eggs and add 1 tablespoon olive oil.

5. For tagliatelle, cut the dough into ¼-inch-wide noodles. Gather the noodles into a few loose nests and sprinkle them with flour. For bowties, cut the dough into 2 by ¾-inch rectangles. Working quickly (before the dough dries), pinch the centers of each rectangle together to form a bowtie. Set the nests or bowties on a floured baking sheet and cover with a clean kitchen towel. Repeat with the remaining half of the dough.

6. Bring a large pot of salted water to a boil. Add the pasta. Cook for 2 to 3 minutes, until the pasta rises to the surface and a sample piece is al dente. Pay close attention to the pasta: like other gluten-free pastas, it can go from perfectly cooked to an overdone, disintegrating mess if you step away.

7. Drain the pasta in a strainer and serve with any pasta sauce of your choice.

storage tip

The pasta can be prepared through step five. Sprinkle the pasta with chickpea flour and refrigerate in an airtight container, separated by sheets of waxed paper, for up to 1 month. Alternatively, sprinkle with flour and freeze in a single layer on a large baking sheet. Transfer the frozen pasta to an airtight container and freeze for up to 3 months (there is no need to defrost prior to using; simply add an additional minute or more to cook).

pumpkin-sage gnocchi

Once you start cooking and baking with chickpea flour, it's easy to understand why I'm crazy about using it in pasta and gnocchi—it adds a subtle, uniquely umami-nutty flavor to almost anything. Here, chickpea flour teams up with pumpkin and sage in a simple-to-prepare gnocchi worthy of busy weeknights. **MAKES 4 SERVINGS**

GNOCCHI

2 cups (240 grams) chickpea flour, plus more for dusting

1 tablespoon whole psyllium husks

1¼ teaspoons dry rubbed sage

¾ teaspoon fine sea salt, plus more for pasta water

¼ teaspoon freshly ground black pepper

1½ cups pumpkin purée (not pie filling)

1 large egg, lightly beaten

2 tablespoons extra-virgin olive oil

SUGGESTED ACCOMPANIMENTS

Good-quality jarred or homemade marinara sauce

Cheese (e.g., grated Parmesan cheese, crumbled blue cheese, crumbled goat cheese)

Nutritional yeast flakes

Chopped fresh, flat-leaf parsley leaves

Melted unsalted butter or ghee

1. In a large bowl, whisk the flour, psyllium husks, sage, salt, and pepper together until blended. Add the pumpkin purée and egg, stirring until completely blended (dough will be stiff). Let stand for 5 minutes.

2. On a clean work surface lightly dusted with chickpea flour, gather the dough together into an even ball; cut into quarters. Roll each quarter of dough into a ¾-inch-thick rope. Repeat with the remaining three quarters of dough. Using a sharp knife, cut the ropes into 1-inch-long gnocchi.

3. To cook, bring a large pot of salted water to a boil. Add half of the gnocchi. Cook for 2 to 3 minutes, until they float to the top of the water. Remove with a slotted spoon and repeat with remaining gnocchi.

4. Heat the oil in a large nonstick skillet set over medium-high heat. Add the gnocchi. Cook for 2 to 3 minutes per side, until browned and slightly crispy. Serve with any of the suggested accompaniments.

VARIATION

Ricotta Chickpea Gnocchi: Omit the sage and replace the pumpkin with an equal amount of ricotta cheese. Add ½ cup freshly grated Parmesan cheese. Reduce the salt to ½ teaspoon.

storage tip

The gnocchi can be prepared through the step of cutting into gnocchi pieces. Sprinkle them with flour and refrigerate in an airtight container, separated by sheets of waxed paper, for up to 1 week. Alternatively, sprinkle with flour and freeze in a single layer on a large baking sheet. Transfer the frozen gnocchi to an airtight container and freeze for up to 3 months (there is no need to defrost prior to using; simply cook until gnocchi float to top of water as directed).

smoky bbq veggie burgers

Serve these on your favorite gluten-free buns, enclose them in a tortilla (page 71) or flatbread (page 72), or use a large piece of lettuce for a fresh and flavorful wrap.

MAKES 4 PATTIES

⅓ cup (40 grams) chickpea flour

1 teaspoon hot smoked paprika (pimentón) or chipotle chile powder

½ teaspoon ground cumin

¾ cup roasted or toasted unsalted sunflower seeds

½ cup packed fresh, flat-leaf parsley leaves

1 (15-ounce) can red kidney beans, rinsed and drained

¼ cup good-quality barbecue sauce

1 to 2 tablespoons water

1 tablespoon olive oil

Lettuce leaves, flatbreads (page 72), or tortillas (page 71), for serving

1. In a large nonstick skillet set over medium-high heat, cook the flour, stirring, for 3 to 4 minutes, until golden brown and fragrant. Add the paprika and cumin; cook, stirring for 30 seconds longer. Transfer to a food processor.

2. Add the sunflower seeds and parsley to the flour and spices in the food processor; process until finely chopped. Add the beans and barbecue sauce; pulse until blended but still chunky. Add 1 to 2 tablespoons water if the mixture appears dry. Let stand for 5 minutes. Form into four ¾-inch-thick patties. Loosely cover and refrigerate for at least 30 minutes until firm.

3. In a large skillet, heat the olive oil over medium-high heat. Add the patties, decrease the heat to medium and cook for 4 minutes. Turn the patties over and cook for 3 to 5 minutes, until crispy on the outside and hot in the center. Serve on lettuce leaves with any of your favorite accompaniments.

tip

The moisture content of canned beans and barbecue sauce can vary. If the patty mixture appears too wet, add a small amount of additional chickpea flour (it need not be toasted); if it seems too dry, add a small amount of water.

VARIATIONS

Za'atar Chickpea Burgers: Use canned chickpeas in place of the kidney beans, cilantro in place of the parsley, and chopped roasted red bell peppers (from a jar, drained) in place of the barbecue sauce. Omit the cumin and add 2 tablespoons za'atar spice blend (page 94) and 2 teaspoons finely grated lemon zest along with the sunflower seeds.

Tex-Mex Black Bean Burgers: Use canned black beans in place of the kidney beans, cilantro in place of the parsley, and thick, prepared tomato salsa in place of the barbecue sauce.

double-crusted samosa pie

In India, vegetable-stuffed samosas are often served as a first course, but baking the crust and filling in a pie pan turns this version into a main course. **MAKES 6 SERVINGS**

CRUST
2½ cups (300 grams) chickpea flour, plus more for dusting
1 teaspoon fine sea salt
5 tablespoons virgin coconut oil, melted
½ cup water

FILLING
1 tablespoon olive oil

1 medium-large onion, finely chopped
4 cups small-diced peeled Yukon Gold or russet potatoes
1 cup small-diced peeled carrots
3 cloves garlic, minced
1½ tablespoons peeled, minced fresh ginger
2 tablespoons medium-heat curry powder

1 teaspoon fine sea salt
1 cup water
1 cup frozen petite green peas
¾ cup well-stirred full-fat coconut milk
½ cup packed fresh cilantro leaves, chopped
Freshly ground black pepper

1. To make the crust, combine the flour and salt in a large bowl. Add the coconut oil and water; stir with a fork until combined. Transfer the dough to a clean work surface dusted with chickpea flour; shape it into 2 equal balls, then flatten each into a disk. Wrap them in plastic wrap and set aside while preparing the filling.

2. To make the filling, heat the olive oil in a large pot set over medium-high heat. Add the onions, potatoes, and carrots; cook and stir for 8 to 10 minutes, until softened. Add the garlic, ginger, curry powder, and salt; cook and stir for 1 minute. Add the water; cover, reduce the heat, and simmer for 8 to 10 minutes, until the potatoes and carrots are very tender. Stir in the peas and coconut milk; cook and stir for 2 minutes. Remove from heat and cool to room temperature. Stir in the cilantro and adjust the salt and pepper to taste.

3. Preheat the oven to 350°F. On a clean work surface lightly dusted with chickpea flour, roll out one of the dough disks into a 10-inch circle; gently press it into a 9-inch pie plate. Spoon the filling into the crust. Roll out the remaining dough in same manner; place it on top of the pie, sealing the top and bottom edges of the crust. Cut 3 to 4 small steam vents in the top with the tip of a sharp knife.

4. Bake for 28 to 33 minutes, until the crust is golden brown. Transfer the pie to a wire rack and cool for 30 minutes. Cut into wedges and serve.

tips
An equal amount of melted unsalted butter or melted unsalted ghee can be used in place of the coconut oil.

If you cannot wait 30 minutes before diving into the pie, keep in mind that it will not cut cleanly into wedges when the filling is very hot.

storage tip
Cover any cooled, leftover pie with plastic wrap and refrigerate it for up to 2 days.

desserts

chocolate chip chickpea cookies

No one will know—or care—that these chocolate chippers are made with chickpea flour. That's because they have everything you expect and love in the quintessential cookie, from the crispy, tender texture to the buttery brown sugar dough to the chunks of chocolate throughout. **MAKES 30 COOKIES**

2 cups (240 grams) chickpea flour

¾ teaspoon baking powder

½ teaspoon baking soda

½ teaspoon fine sea salt

1⅔ cups packed light brown sugar

8 tablespoons (1 stick) unsalted butter, softened

2 large eggs

1 teaspoon vanilla extract

8 ounces semisweet chocolate, coarsely chopped

1. In a medium bowl, whisk together the flour, baking powder, baking soda, and salt.

2. In another medium bowl, using an electric mixer, beat the brown sugar and butter on medium speed for 1 to 2 minutes, until light and fluffy. Scrape the sides and bottom of the bowl with a rubber spatula. Add the eggs and vanilla; beat for 1 minute, until blended and smooth. Stir in the flour mixture (by hand) until just blended; stir in the chocolate chips.

3. Tightly cover the bowl with plastic wrap and refrigerate the dough for 1 hour or up to 24 hours.

4. Preheat the oven to 325°F. Line a large baking sheet with parchment paper.

5. Scoop heaping tablespoons of dough 2 inches apart onto the prepared baking sheet.

6. Bake for 15 to 20 minutes, until just set at the edges (centers will be slightly soft). Let cool on the pan on a wire rack for 2 minutes, then transfer directly onto the rack with a spatula to cool completely.

tips

Place the cookie dough back into the refrigerator between batches.

An equal amount of coconut palm sugar can be used in place of the brown sugar.

You can use 1⅓ cups semisweet chocolate chips in place of the chopped chocolate.

make it vegan!

Replace the eggs with 2 psyllium "eggs" (page 18) and replace the butter with nonhydrogenated organic vegetable shortening.

storage tip

Store the cooled cookies in an airtight container in the refrigerator for up to 5 days or in the freezer for up to 2 months.

cranberry & pepita biscotti

It's the combination of crunchy green pepitas and ruby-hued, tart-sweet cranberries that really sell these biscotti. Olive oil is a traditional component of classic Italian biscotti, yielding cookies that are just the right balance of crisp and tender. **MAKES 40 COOKIES**

1¾ cups (210 grams) chickpea flour
1¼ teaspoons baking powder
¼ teaspoon fine sea salt

¾ cup natural cane sugar
2 large eggs
¼ cup extra-virgin olive oil

2 teaspoons vanilla extract
¾ cup pepitas (green pumpkin seeds)
½ cup dried cranberries

1. Preheat the oven to 300°F. Line a large baking sheet with parchment paper.

2. In a medium bowl, whisk together the flour, baking powder, and salt.

3. In a large bowl, whisk together the sugar, eggs, oil, and vanilla until blended. Add the flour mixture, pepitas, and cranberries, stirring until just blended.

4. Divide the dough in half and place both halves on the prepared baking sheet. Using moistened hands, shape into two parallel 12 by 2-inch rectangles, spaced about 3 inches apart.

5. Bake for 30 to 35 minutes, until golden and the centers are set. Let cool on the pan on a wire rack for 15 minutes.

6. Cut each rectangle crosswise at a slight diagonal into ½- to ¾-inch slices. Place the slices flat, cut sides down, on the baking sheet. Bake for 8 to 10 minutes, until the edges are dark golden. Let the biscotti cool completely on the pan.

tips

If you do not have any nut concerns, feel free to use an equal amount of chopped nuts (e.g., almonds, pecans, or hazelnuts) in place of the pepitas.

The biscotti will continue to harden after the second bake as they cool.

make it vegan!
Replace the eggs with 2 psyllium "eggs" (page 18).

storage tip
Store the cooled biscotti in an airtight container at room temperature for up to 5 days.

VARIATIONS

Tart Cherry Chocolate Chunk Biscotti: Replace the pepitas with 4 ounces chopped semisweet chocolate and replace the cranberries with an equal amount of chopped dried tart cherries.

Lemon Ginger Biscotti: Add 1 teaspoon ground ginger to the flour mixture. Replace the vanilla with 2½ teaspoons finely grated lemon zest. Replace the pepitas and cranberries with ⅔ cup chopped candied (crystallized) ginger.

cardamom vanilla shortbread

Shortbread is, was, and always will be one of my favorite cookies, so I persevered in creating a version with chickpea flour. My son knew about my quest (he tasted—and promptly rejected—many of my earlier attempts), but when he tried one of these cardamom-vanilla beauties, he had three words: "Nailed it, Mommy!" **MAKES 16 COOKIES**

2½ cups (300 grams) chickpea flour
¾ teaspoon ground cardamom

½ teaspoon fine sea salt
2 sticks (1 cup) unsalted butter, softened

½ cup natural cane sugar
2 teaspoons vanilla extract

1. Line an 8-inch square pan with parchment paper, leaving a 2-inch overhang on two opposing sides. In a medium bowl, whisk together the flour, cardamom, and salt.

2. In another medium bowl, cream the butter and sugar together with a wooden spoon until completely blended and smooth; stir in the vanilla until blended. Stir in the flour mixture until a cohesive dough forms.

3. Press the dough into the prepared pan. Tightly cover the pan with plastic wrap and refrigerate the dough for 1 hour or up to 24 hours.

4. Preheat the oven to 325°F. Line a large baking sheet with parchment paper.

5. Holding on to the parchment paper, lift the dough out of the baking pan and transfer to a cutting board. Cut it into 16 squares. Place the squares 2 inches apart on the prepared baking sheet.

6. Bake for 15 to 20 minutes, until pale golden. Transfer the cookies directly onto a cooling rack to cool completely.

tips

If desired, prick several small holes (with a toothpick or wooden skewer) into the surface of each cookie before baking. This is purely decorative and does not alter the texture or baking time of the shortbread.

If you do not have an 8-inch square baking pan, simply roll or press the dough into an 8-inch square on a piece of parchment paper.

make it vegan!
Replace the butter with virgin coconut oil, softened (but not melted).

VARIATIONS

Scottish Shortbread: Omit the cardamom.

Coconut Sugar Shortbread: Omit the cardamom and vanilla. Replace the cane sugar with an equal amount of coconut palm sugar.

molasses spice cookies

I cannot imagine the winter holidays without a batch—or several—of molasses spice cookies. This rendition tastes both traditional and absolutely delicious, especially because—not in spite—of the use of chickpea flour, which happens to be a great match for bold spices and the rich, caramel notes of molasses. MAKES 48 COOKIES

2½ cups (300 grams) chickpea flour
1 tablespoon ground ginger
2¼ teaspoons baking soda
1 teaspoon ground cinnamon

½ teaspoon fine sea salt
¼ teaspoon ground cloves
½ cup coconut palm sugar or packed light brown sugar
½ cup natural cane sugar, plus more for rolling

¾ cup (1½ sticks) unsalted butter, softened
1 large egg
6 tablespoons dark molasses (not blackstrap)

1. In a medium bowl, whisk together the flour, ginger, baking soda, cinnamon, salt, and cloves.

2. In another medium bowl, using an electric mixer, beat the coconut sugar, ½ cup cane sugar, and the butter on medium speed for 1 to 2 minutes, until light and fluffy. Scrape the sides and bottom of the bowl with a rubber spatula. Add the egg and molasses; beat for 1 minute, until blended and smooth. Stir in the flour mixture by hand until just blended.

3. Tightly cover the bowl with plastic wrap and refrigerate the dough for 1 hour or up to 24 hours.

4. Preheat the oven to 325°F. Line a large baking sheet with parchment paper.

5. Fill a small, shallow plate with natural cane sugar. Roll tablespoons of dough into balls and then roll in sugar to coat. Place 2 inches apart on the prepared baking sheet.

6. Bake for 14 to 19 minutes, until the tops are cracked and the edges are set (centers will be slightly soft). Let cool on the pan on a wire rack for 3 minutes, then transfer directly onto the rack with a spatula to cool completely.

tip
Place the cookie dough back into the refrigerator between batches.

make it vegan!
Replace the egg with a psyllium "egg" (page 18) and replace the butter with nonhydrogenated organic vegetable shortening.

storage tip
Store the cooled cookies in an airtight container in the refrigerator for up to 5 days or in the freezer for up to 2 months.

tahini & jam thumbprints

If you love tahini in all forms, as I do, you will love these simple, jam-filled cookies. They have a not-too-sweet flavor reminiscent of sesame halvah, and a tender, melt-in-your-mouth texture. The dot of jam in the center is a fruit-sweet bonus.

MAKES 24 COOKIES

¾ cup well-stirred tahini
¾ cup natural cane sugar
1 large egg

1 teaspoon vanilla extract
⅛ teaspoon fine sea salt

⅓ cup (40 grams) chickpea flour
¼ cup fruit jam (any variety)

1. In a medium bowl, using an electric mixer, beat the tahini, sugar, egg, vanilla, and salt on medium speed for 1 to 2 minutes, until light and fluffy. Scrape the sides and bottom of the bowl with a rubber spatula. Stir in the flour by hand until just blended.

2. Line a large cookie sheet with parchment paper. Shape the dough into 24 1-inch balls; place them 1 inch apart on the prepared cookie sheet. Press your thumb into the center of each cookie, leaving an indentation. Loosely cover the pan and refrigerate for at least 2 hours.

3. Preheat the oven to 325°F.

4. Bake the cookies for 10 to 12 minutes, until pale golden. Transfer to a wire rack with a spatula and cool completely. Spoon ½ teaspoon jam into the center of each cookie and serve.

tips

Be careful not to overbake the cookies; they will become firm as they cool.

An equal amount of coconut palm sugar can be used in place of the cane sugar.

An equal amount of sunflower seed butter or hemp seed butter can be used in place of the tahini. If you do not have any nut concerns, feel free to use an equal amount of nut butter (e.g., peanut or almond).

make it vegan!

Replace the egg with a psyllium "egg" (page 18).

storage tip

Store the cooled cookies in an airtight container in the refrigerator for up to 5 days or in the freezer for up to 2 months.

chocolate fudge saucepan brownies

Rich with chocolate flavor and laden with old-fashioned charm, these fudgy brownies will make you swoon. Gluten-free, grain-free chickpea flour makes for an especially smooth, truffle-like texture and heightens the earthy flavors of the cocoa powder.

MAKES 16 BROWNIES

Nonstick cooking spray
½ cup (1 stick) unsalted butter, cut into small pieces
2 tablespoons neutral vegetable oil

1 cup coconut palm sugar or natural cane sugar
¾ cup unsweetened natural cocoa powder
1 teaspoon vanilla extract

2 large eggs
⅓ cup (40 grams) chickpea flour
¼ teaspoon baking soda
¼ teaspoon fine sea salt

1. Preheat the oven to 325°F. Line an 8-inch square baking pan with parchment paper, leaving a 2-inch overhang on two opposing sides. Spray the paper with nonstick cooking spray.

2. In a medium saucepan, melt the stick of butter over medium heat. Add the oil, sugar, and cocoa powder; cook and stir for 1 minute longer. Remove from the heat and whisk in the vanilla; cool for 5 minutes.

make it vegan!
Replace the eggs with 2 psyllium "eggs" (page 18) and replace the butter with virgin coconut oil.

3. Add the eggs to the cocoa mixture, whisking vigorously until the mixture is blended and appears thick and glossy. Add the flour, baking soda, and salt; whisk vigorously for 30 seconds. Spread the batter in the prepared pan.

4. Bake the brownies for 23 to 28 minutes, until a toothpick inserted into the center comes out with a few moist crumbs attached. Transfer the pan to a wire rack; cool completely in the pan.

5. Holding on to the paper, lift the brownies from the pan. Remove the paper and cut into 16 squares.

browned butter blondies

Here is one of my favorite desserts, made brand new—and dare I say, even better—with chickpea flour. Browning the butter lends a glorious, nutty flavor that marries beautifully with the chickpea flour and caramel-like coconut sugar, but melted ghee or melted virgin coconut oil yields delicious results as well. **MAKES 20 BLONDIES**

Nonstick cooking spray

1½ cups (180 grams) chickpea flour

2 teaspoons baking powder

1 teaspoon fine sea salt

2 cups coconut palm sugar

½ cup (1 stick) unsalted butter, cut into small pieces

2 large eggs

2 teaspoons vanilla extract

¾ cup semisweet chocolate chips

1. Preheat the oven to 350°F. Line a 9-inch square baking pan with parchment paper leaving a slight overhang on two opposing sides; spray the paper and sides of the pan with nonstick cooking spray.

2. In a medium bowl, whisk together the flour, baking powder, and salt. Place the sugar in a large bowl.

3. In a small saucepan, melt the stick of butter over medium heat. Continue to cook the butter, swirling the pan several times, for 5 minutes, until it starts to brown. Remove from heat and cool slightly. Whisk the browned butter into the sugar until blended; whisk in the eggs and vanilla. Add the flour mixture, stirring until just blended; stir in the chocolate chips.

4. Spread the batter into the prepared pan. Bake for 40 to 45 minutes, until a toothpick comes out with a few moist crumbs attached. Transfer to a wire rack and cool completely in the pan. Holding on to the paper, remove the blondies from the pan. Remove the paper and cut into pieces.

make it vegan!

Replace the eggs with 2 psyllium "eggs" (page 18) and replace the butter with virgin coconut oil. Do not attempt to brown the oil; simply melt the oil over low heat.

peach cobbler cake

Part pie, part cake, and 100 percent delicious, this dessert offers three distinct textures and flavors: vanilla-scented cake, luscious fruit, and a crisp, coconut topping. **MAKES 8 SERVINGS**

3 cups sliced peeled peaches (about 1 pound)

8 tablespoons natural cane sugar

2 teaspoons fresh lemon juice

4 tablespoons unsalted butter

¾ cup (90 grams) chickpea flour

1½ teaspoons baking powder

¼ teaspoon ground allspice

¼ teaspoon baking soda

⅛ teaspoon fine sea salt

¾ cup buttermilk

1 teaspoon vanilla extract

⅓ cup unsweetened flaked coconut, chopped

1. Preheat the oven to 325°F.

2. In a 9-inch cast iron skillet or other oven-proof skillet, combine the peaches, 2 tablespoons of the sugar, and the lemon juice. Cook and stir over medium heat until the sugar is melted and begins to bubble; scrape the mixture into a medium bowl and wipe out the skillet.

3. In the same skillet, melt the butter over medium heat. Remove from the heat.

4. In another medium bowl, whisk together the flour, 5 tablespoons sugar, the baking powder, allspice, baking soda, and salt; add the buttermilk and vanilla, whisking until just blended.

5. Spoon the batter into the skillet with the melted butter, spreading it evenly with a spatula without mixing in the butter. Spoon the peaches, including all the juices, evenly over the batter. Sprinkle with the coconut and the remaining tablespoon of sugar.

6. Bake for 45 to 50 minutes, until golden brown. Transfer to a wire rack to cool for at least 15 minutes. Serve warm.

make it vegan!
Replace the butter with virgin coconut oil and use nondairy buttermilk (page 21).

VARIATIONS

Peach Melba Cobbler Cake: Reduce the amount of peaches to 2 cups and add 1 cup raspberries.

Blackberry Cobbler Cake: Replace the peaches with 3 cups blackberries.

double chocolate cake

Chocolate cake is an American icon, and this one lives up to—and then exceeds—expectations. The humble list of ingredients makes it easy to concoct at a moment's notice, which is a wonderful thing indeed. **MAKES 9 SERVINGS**

½ cup neutral vegetable oil, plus more for pan

1½ cups (180 grams) chickpea flour

¾ cup natural cane sugar

⅓ cup unsweetened natural cocoa powder

¾ teaspoon baking soda

½ teaspoon fine sea salt

1 cup water

2 teaspoons cider vinegar or white vinegar

2 teaspoons vanilla extract

⅓ cup miniature chocolate chips

1. Preheat the oven to 350°F. Line a 9-inch square metal baking pan with parchment paper leaving a 2-inch overhang on two opposing sides. Grease the paper and sides of the pan with vegetable oil.

2. In a large bowl, whisk together the flour, sugar, cocoa powder, baking soda, and salt.

3. In a medium bowl, whisk the water, ½ cup vegetable oil, vinegar, and vanilla.

4. Add the water mixture to the flour mixture, stirring until just blended. Immediately pour the batter into the prepared pan; sprinkle with chocolate chips.

5. Bake for 25 to 30 minutes, until a toothpick inserted in the center comes out clean. Cool it completely in the pan on a wire rack. Holding on to the paper, lift the cake from the pan. Remove the paper, cut into pieces, and serve.

storage tip

Store the cooled cake, loosely wrapped in foil or waxed paper, at room temperature for up to 1 week. Alternatively, wrap it in plastic wrap, then foil, completely enclosing the cake, and freeze for up to 6 months. Let thaw at room temperature for 4 to 6 hours before serving.

apple pie cake

As much as I love apple pie, this easy alternative—buttery cake swaddling rows of tart-sweet apple slices—is one of my favorite alternatives. **MAKES 8 SERVINGS**

Nonstick cooking spray
3 medium-large (about 1¼ pounds) tart-sweet apples
3 tablespoons natural cane sugar, divided
½ teaspoon ground cinnamon

1⅓ cups (160 grams) chickpea flour
2 teaspoons baking powder
½ teaspoon fine sea salt
6 tablespoons unsalted butter, softened

1 cup coconut palm sugar or packed light brown sugar
1 large egg
1 teaspoon vanilla extract
¼ cup milk

1. Preheat the oven to 350°F. Line a 9-inch square metal baking pan with parchment paper, leaving a 2-inch overhang on two opposing sides. Spray the paper and sides of the pan with nonstick cooking spray.

2. Peel, core, and slice the apples ¼-inch thick; place the slices in a large bowl. Add 2 tablespoons of the cane sugar and cinnamon, tossing to combine.

3. In a small bowl, whisk together the flour, baking powder, and salt.

4. In a medium bowl, beat the butter and coconut sugar with an electric mixer on medium speed until light and fluffy. Add the egg, beating until well blended. Mix in the vanilla.

5. Alternate adding the milk and flour mixture, a small amount at a time, with the mixer on low speed, until just blended.

6. Spread the batter evenly in the prepared pan. Arrange the apple slices over the batter, gently pressing them into the batter. Sprinkle with remaining cane sugar.

7. Bake for 45 to 50 minutes, until the apples are tender and a toothpick inserted into the center comes out clean. Let it cool completely in the pan on a wire rack. Holding on to the paper, lift the cake from the pan. Remove the paper, cut into pieces, and serve.

VARIATION

Italian Plum Cake: Replace the apples with 1 pound of plums (preferably Italian plums) that have been pitted and quartered.

tips
For the apples, consider using Gala, Braeburn, or Golden Delicious.

You can use either fine- or coarse-grain natural cane sugar.

make it vegan!
Replace the egg with a psyllium "egg" (page 18) and replace the butter with virgin coconut oil. Use nondairy milk.

fresh ginger gingerbread

Is there anything better than the scent of gingerbread baking when it's cold and damp outside? Wait, let me answer that: no, there simply isn't. And this dark, moist, fragrant cake will have everyone fighting over the last piece. MAKES 9 SERVINGS

Nonstick cooking spray
1¼ cups (150 grams) chickpea flour
1 teaspoon ground cinnamon
¼ teaspoon ground cloves

½ teaspoon baking soda
¼ teaspoon fine sea salt
1½ tablespoons peeled, grated fresh ginger
1 large egg
½ cup buttermilk

½ cup dark molasses (not blackstrap)
⅓ cup neutral vegetable oil
⅓ cup coconut palm sugar or packed light brown sugar

1. Preheat the oven to 350°F. Line an 8-inch square metal baking pan with parchment paper, leaving a 2-inch overhang on two opposing sides. Spray the paper and sides of the pan with nonstick cooking spray.

2. In a large bowl, whisk together the flour, cinnamon, cloves, baking soda, and salt.

3. Add the ginger, egg, buttermilk, molasses, oil, and coconut sugar to the flour mixture. Using an electric mixer on medium-low speed, beat for 1 minute, until blended. Scrape the sides and bottom of the bowl with a rubber spatula. Beat on medium speed for 1 minute more.

4. Spread the batter evenly in the prepared pan. Bake for 25 to 30 minutes, until a toothpick inserted in the center comes out with a few moist crumbs attached. Let cool completely in the pan on a wire rack. Holding on to the paper overhang, remove the cake from the pan. Cut into squares and serve.

tip
For a milder-flavored cake, use pure maple syrup or honey in place of the molasses.

make it vegan!
Replace the egg with a psyllium "egg" (page 18) and replace the buttermilk with nondairy buttermilk (page 21).

storage tip
Store the cooled cake loosely wrapped in foil or parchment paper in the refrigerator for up to 5 days. Alternatively, wrap it in plastic wrap, then foil, completely enclosing the cake, and freeze for up to 6 months. Let thaw at room temperature for 4 to 6 hours before serving.

flaky, no-roll pie crust

No rolling. No lining with foil. No weighting with beans. No kidding! Have fun filling this buttery, flaky crust with all of your favorite fillings. **MAKES ONE 9-INCH PIE CRUST**

1½ cups (180 grams) chickpea flour

2 tablespoons natural cane sugar

¾ teaspoon fine sea salt

⅛ teaspoon baking powder

5 tablespoons unsalted butter, softened

¼ cup neutral vegetable oil

2 tablespoons milk

1. In a medium bowl, whisk together the flour, sugar, salt, and baking powder. Add the butter, oil, and milk to the bowl; stir until well blended.

2. Evenly press the dough onto the bottom and sides of a 9-inch pie plate. Loosely cover with plastic wrap and refrigerate for at least 1 hour or freeze for 20 minutes.

3. Preheat the oven to 325°F. To parbake the crust, bake for 10 to 15 minutes, until pale golden. Let it cool slightly on a wire rack, then fill and bake as directed in the pie recipe.

4. To bake completely, bake for 20 to 25 minutes, until light golden brown and set at the edges. Let it cool completely on a wire rack. Fill as desired.

make it vegan!
Replace the butter with an equal amount of nonhydrogenated organic vegetable shortening. Use nondairy milk.

maple spice pumpkin pie

Pumpkin, maple syrup, and coconut milk form an irresistible autumn trinity in my new take on classic pumpkin pie. **MAKES ONE 9-INCH PIE**

1 tablespoon pumpkin
  pie spice
½ teaspoon fine sea salt
2 large eggs
1 (15-ounce) can
  pumpkin purée (not
  pie filling)

⅔ cup pure maple syrup
1 cup well-stirred full-fat
  coconut milk
1 parbaked Flaky,
  No-Roll Pie Crust
  (page 163)

Whipped Coconut
  Cream, for serving
  (optional; page 170)

1. Preheat the oven to 325°F. In a large bowl, whisk together the pumpkin pie spice, salt, eggs, pumpkin, maple syrup, and coconut milk until well blended. Spread the filling in the crust.

2. Bake for 60 to 70 minutes, until the center is set. Let cool completely on a wire rack. Serve at room temperature or refrigerate until ready to serve. Serve topped with whipped coconut cream, if desired.

make it vegan!
Use the vegan version of the flaky pie crust. For the filling, replace the eggs with ⅓ cup well-stirred tahini and 2 teaspoons whole psyllium husks.

storage tip
Store the cooled pie, loosely wrapped in foil or waxed paper, in the refrigerator for up to 3 days.

chickpea fudge

This fudge is my take on *besan ki barfi*, a popular chickpea-flour confection enjoyed in India, Pakistan, and Iran. I've cut down on much of the sugar found in classic recipes but have kept one of the classic flavorings: cardamom. **MAKES 16 PIECES**

Nonstick cooking spray
1 cup (120 grams) chickpea flour
½ cup (1 stick) unsalted butter, melted

⅔ cup coconut palm sugar
¼ cup water
½ teaspoon ground cardamom

⅛ teaspoon fine sea salt
2 tablespoons toasted or raw seeds (such as pepitas, chia seeds, or sesame seeds; optional)

1. Line an 8 by 4-inch loaf pan with parchment paper or foil, leaving a 2-inch overhang on two opposing sides; spray the parchment and sides with nonstick cooking spray.

2. In a large nonstick skillet, toast the flour over medium heat, stirring constantly, for 3 to 4 minutes, until the color darkens slightly and the flour begins to smell nutty.

3. Add the butter to the skillet with the flour. Continue to cook, stirring (the mixture will appear dry and crumbly at first), for 3 to 5 minutes, until it looks like thick, dark golden gravy. Scrape into a medium bowl. Wipe out the skillet.

4. Add the sugar, water, cardamom, and salt to the same skillet. Cook and stir for 4 to 6 minutes, until the sugar is melted and the mixture has thickened slightly.

5. Return the chickpea flour mixture to the skillet. Cook and stir over medium heat for 3 to 4 minutes, until thick and creamy. Spread in the prepared pan, smoothing the top. Sprinkle with seeds, gently pressing into the fudge.

6. Loosely cover the fudge and refrigerate for at least 3 hours, until cold and firm. Hold on to the parchment to remove the fudge. Peel off the parchment and cut into small squares.

tip
An equal amount of natural cane sugar or packed light brown sugar can be used in place of the coconut sugar.

make it vegan!
Use an equal amount of virgin coconut oil, melted, in place of the butter.

storage tip
Store in an airtight container in the refrigerator for up to 2 weeks, or in the freezer for up to 3 months.

VARIATION

Toasted Coconut Fudge: Omit the cardamom and replace the butter with an equal amount of virgin coconut oil (melted). In place of the seeds, sprinkle top of fudge with ⅓ cup toasted unsweetened flaked coconut.

mocha cream pie

The classic combination of chocolate and coffee becomes new again when paired with luscious coconut milk. **MAKES ONE 9-INCH PIE**

12 ounces semisweet chocolate, chopped

2 cups well-stirred full-fat coconut milk

1 tablespoon instant espresso powder

2 teaspoons vanilla extract

¼ teaspoon fine sea salt

1 completely baked Flaky, No-Roll Pie Crust (page 163)

1½ cups Whipped Coffee Coconut Cream (page 170)

Semisweet chocolate shavings, for garnish (optional)

1. Place the chocolate in a large bowl.

2. In a medium saucepan, heat the coconut milk and espresso powder over medium heat until hot but not boiling; pour it over the chocolate. Let stand for 2 minutes. Add the vanilla and salt, then whisk until blended and smooth. Let cool at room temperature for 30 minutes.

3. Whisk the filling and pour it into the baked pie crust. Lay plastic wrap directly on the surface of the filling and refrigerate for at least 3 hours, until set.

4. Remove the plastic wrap and spread coconut cream over the chilled pie filling. Sprinkle with chocolate shavings, if desired.

tip
2 cups of semisweet chocolate chips can be used in place of the chopped chocolate.

make it vegan!
Use the vegan version of the flaky pie crust.

storage tip
Prepare the pie through step 3 and store, loosely wrapped in foil or waxed paper, in the refrigerator for up to 2 days.

blueberry crisp

Chickpea flour and coconut palm sugar create a golden-crisp topping for lush blueberries. Chia seeds are terrific here, and in other desserts, for thickening the filling without starches or gums. If you don't like the texture of the seeds, simply crush them with a mortar and pestle before adding. **MAKES 8 SERVINGS**

TOPPING
8 tablespoons (1 stick) cold unsalted butter, cut into small pieces, plus more for pan
1⅓ cups (160 grams) chickpea flour
⅓ cup coconut palm sugar

½ teaspoon baking powder
⅛ teaspoon fine sea salt
1 teaspoon vanilla extract

FILLING
¼ cup coconut palm sugar

1½ tablespoons chia seeds
2 teaspoons freshly grated lemon zest
1½ tablespoons fresh lemon juice
¼ teaspoon fine sea salt
6 cups fresh or frozen (thawed) blueberries

1. Preheat the oven to 325°F. Grease a 9-inch square baking dish with butter.

2. To make the topping, whisk the flour, sugar, baking powder, and salt together in a medium bowl. Add the stick of butter and vanilla; using your fingers or a pastry cutter, work in the butter until the mixture resembles coarse breadcrumbs. Place the bowl in the freezer for 10 minutes while you prepare the filling.

3. To make the filling, combine the sugar, chia seeds, lemon zest, lemon juice, and salt in a large bowl. Add the blueberries, gently tossing to coat. Transfer the filling to the prepared dish; sprinkle evenly with the topping.

4. Bake for 45 to 50 minutes, until the topping is golden and appears dry and the filling is bubbling. Check the crisp at 30 minutes. If the topping already appears golden, cover the pan with foil to prevent over-browning. Transfer to a wire rack and cool until warm or completely cooled.

tip
An equal amount of packed light brown sugar can be used in place of the coconut palm sugar.

make it vegan!
Use an equal amount of cold virgin coconut oil in place of the butter.

whipped coconut cream

It's hard to imagine that anything can beat billowy whipped cream as a dessert topping, but whipped coconut cream can and does. It's wonderful straight up, but you can use a bit of sweetener or any flavorings you might add to whipped cream (e.g., vanilla extract or citrus zest), too. **MAKES ABOUT ¾ CUP**

1 (14-ounce) can full-fat
  coconut milk

1. Refrigerate the can of coconut milk for at least 24 hours.

2. Just before whipping the coconut cream, place a medium bowl (preferably metal) and the beaters from the electric mixer in the freezer for 5 minutes.

3. Remove the can from the refrigerator. Flip the can upside down and open from the bottom end. Pour off the liquid (store the liquid in an airtight container in the refrigerator for another use). Scoop the thick coconut cream into the chilled bowl.

4. Whip the coconut cream with an electric mixer on high until soft peaks form. Use immediately.

VARIATIONS

Whipped Coffee Coconut Cream: Dissolve 1½ teaspoons instant espresso powder in 1½ teaspoons vanilla extract. Add the espresso-vanilla mixture and 2 teaspoons natural cane sugar near the end of whipping.

Whipped Lemon Coconut Cream: Add 2 teaspoons natural cane sugar, 1½ teaspoons finely grated lemon zest, and 1 tablespoon fresh lemon juice near the end of whipping.

Whipped Vanilla Coconut Cream: Add 2 teaspoons natural cane sugar and 1 teaspoon vanilla extract near the end of whipping.

tip

Some brands of coconut milk have added whitening agents (such as potassium metabisulfate) and/or emulsifiers (such as guar gum, carrageenan, methyl cellulose, or cornstarch) that prevent separation of the coconut fats and liquid. Making whipped coconut cream may not be possible with brands containing more than one of these additives because the cream will not solidify properly when chilled. I find that the brands with guar gum as the only additive tend to work fine. These include such brands as Native Forest Organic, A Taste of Thai, and Aroy-D.

storage tip

Store any unused whipped coconut cream in an airtight container in the refrigerator for up to 2 weeks. Rewhip with an electric mixer before using.

ingredient sources

Gluten-Free Chickpea (Garbanzo Bean) Flour Producers

BARRY FARM
www.barryfarm.com

Barry Farm processes their chickpea flour (Garbanzo Bean Flour on their site) in a separate, gluten-free facility and offers it for sale in bulk quantities to your specification.

Barry Farm is also a good source for bulk quantities of natural cane sugar (Cane Juice Crystals on their site), seeds (raw pepitas, sunflower seeds, and sesame seeds), herbs, spices, and unsulfured dried fruit.

BOB'S RED MILL
www.bobsredmill.com

Bob's Red Mill processes their chickpea flour (Garbanzo Bean Flour on their site) in a separate, gluten-free facility and offers it for sale in 1-pound bags. It is the most widely available brand at supermarkets, natural food stores, and online sites.

Bob's Red Mill is also an excellent source for gluten-free leaveners (baking powder and baking soda), flaxseed meal, seeds (chia seeds, sesame seeds, and pepitas), and dried fruit.

Additional Ingredient Sources

ARTISANA ORGANIC FOODS
www.artisanafoods.com

Producer of raw, organic nut and seed butters as well as organic, raw, extra-virgin coconut oil.

EDEN FOODS
www.edenfoods.com

An excellent source for high-quality, organic ingredients including spices, expeller-pressed cooking oils, and dried fruit.

FLORIDA CRYSTALS
www.floridacrystals.com

Producer of a broad spectrum of minimally processed natural cane sugars, all of which are free of preservatives and artificial ingredients.

MARANATHA FOODS
www.maranathafoods.com

Producer of minimally processed nut and seed butters, including many organic and raw options.

NAVITAS NATURALS
www.navitasnaturals.com

Purveyor of certified organic, minimally processed superfoods such as chia seeds, hemp hearts, cacao nibs, flaxseed meal, and goji berries.

NUTS.COM
www.nuts.com

One-stop online shop for bulk foods—including many organic options—such as nuts, seeds (e.g., hemp, chia, pepita), dried fruits, organic natural cane sugars, organic unsweetened nut butters, coconut, and more. Nuts.com sells chickpea flour in bulk at excellent prices, but it is not certified gluten-free.

PENZEYS SPICES
www.penzeys.com

A shop with an unmatched variety of spices, extracts, and sea salts, all at excellent prices.

SPECTRUM ORGANICS
www.spectrumorganics.com

Producer of expeller-pressed cooking oils (many of which are organic), coconut oil, and cooking sprays made without chlorofluorocarbons.

SUNSPIRE
www.sunspire.com

Producer of high-quality dairy-free (vegan) and gluten-free chocolate chips and baking chocolate.

WHOLESOME SWEETENERS
www.wholesomesweeteners.com

Producer of agave nectar, honey, and natural cane sugars made without bleaching agents or bone char.

VITACOST
www.vitacost.com

One-stop shopping for almost every ingredient you need for making the recipes in this collection—all at discount prices—including chickpea flour, natural nut and seed butters, organic spices, minimally processed sweeteners, and so much more.

acknowledgments

First, I would like to thank my husband Kevin, who routinely ignored the piles of bowls in the sink, chickpea flour on floors and counters, and batter in my hair as I worked to meet my deadlines. Also, to my son Nick, who waited on countless occasions—usually for longer than I promised—for me to finish mixing, baking, or sautéing "just one more batch" of a chickpea flour recipe before we could play.

Thanks also to my friends, especially those in my Wednesday night dinner group, who sampled and provided feedback for many of my creations. Just seeing all of you each week made even the longest work weeks special.

Working with Hiroko, Jenn and Pimpila at Lake Isle Press is not only a privilege, but a joy. Their enthusiasm, wisdom, and warmth, coupled with keen savvy and eyes for detail, makes life as a food writer and recipe developer a pleasure.

index